UNDER THE BRIGHT SKY

01 02 03 04 05 25 24 23 22 21

Caitlin Press Inc.
8100 Alderwood Road
Halfmoon Bay, BC V0N 1Y1
www.caitlin-press.com

Edited by Meg Yamamoto.
Text and cover design by Vici Johnstone.
Photos from the author's collection, unless otherwise noted.
Copyright Andrew Scott.
Cover photo: Stilt fishing at Unawatuna, Sri Lanka. Copyright Katherine Johnston.
Printed in Canada.

Caitlin Press Inc. acknowledges financial support from the Government of Canada and the Canada Council for the Arts, and the Province of British Columbia through the British Columbia Arts Council and the Book Publisher's Tax Credit.

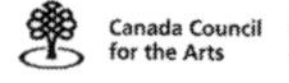

Library and Archives Canada Cataloguing in Publication

Under the bright sky : a memoir of travels through Asia / Andrew Scott.
Scott, Andrew, 1947- author.
Canadiana 20210200502 | ISBN 9781773860619 (softcover)
LCSH: Travelers—Asia—Anecdotes. | LCSH: Asia—Description and travel—Anecdotes. | LCSH: Voyages and travels—Anecdotes.
LCC DS5.95 .S36 2021 | DDC 915.04—dc23

Under the Bright Sky

A Memoir of Travels Through Asia

Andrew Scott

Caitlin Press

2021

More publications by Andrew Scott

The Promise of Paradise:
Utopian Communities in British Columbia

The Encyclopedia of Raincoast Place Names:
A Complete Reference to Coastal British Columbia

The People's Water:
The Fight for the Sunshine Coast's Drinking Watersheds
(with Daniel Bouman)

Painter, Paddler:
The Art and Adventures of Stewart Marshall

Secret Coastline II:
More Journeys and Discoveries along BC's Shores

Secret Coastline:
Journeys and Discoveries along BC's Shores

For Katherine

Fellow traveller

Arriving at Alappuzha by ferry at dusk, Kerala, India.

Contents

Prologue

These stories begin, as stories often do, with an unexpected encounter. It was 1974, an evening in September. I was getting ready to head across town when the sister of a friend asked if she could get a ride with me. Sure, no problem, hop aboard, I'd said, and soon the pair of us were rolling down Fourth Avenue, chatting amiably about our respective jobs. That ride was over far too soon for me.

I scarcely knew my passenger. Indeed I'd almost forgotten that my friend even had a sister. Shiane was her name, and she worked as a graphic artist for one of Vancouver's leading design studios. In less than half an hour, perched on the front seat of my Volkswagen van, looking as sleek and comfortable as a cat, she proceeded to cast an inexplicable spell on me. As we closed in on her destination, I searched for a not-too-obvious way of seeing her again. But she told me she was involved with someone, so I tried, with difficulty, to put her out of my mind.

The fact that Shiane and I were of different ethnicities was irrelevant to me. She was Chinese Canadian, I was white, and Vancouver was in the long, slow process of

Opposite: Sukhothai Historical Park, Thailand.

transforming itself from a predominantly white community to one that was multiracial and multicultural. The city was becoming worldly as well as scenic, and I felt some of that worldliness rub off on me. At work, for instance, as a shiny new employee of Canada Post, I found myself mixing with a much more diverse assortment of people than I was used to. The experience was daunting but also intriguing, a constant challenge to my many preconceived notions.

I'd been hired as a mail service courier. Like a swarm of colourful bees, the couriers would emerge from the huge downtown processing plant that was our corporate hive and spread out through the city each weekday morning. In gleaming red-white-and-blue vans, we cleared mailboxes, set out bags for letter carriers, delivered parcels and express envelopes, and handled airport runs. My task was to fill in for sick or vacationing drivers, a role that older couriers didn't want, preferring a regular beat. But I enjoyed the variety of working in a different part of the city each day, and I kept at it—on and off, part-time and full-time—for several years. That job helped me survive as I slowly built a modest career as a freelance writer and, later, as a magazine editor.

Many of my fellow couriers were Chinese Canadian, and I soon got to know a few of them. I was pleased to have Asian friends. It felt like a standard progression, no big deal, in a place like Vancouver, where Chinese people had always been an important part of urban life. By the mid-1970s, while I was working as a postie, the city's Chinese population had passed the thirty-thousand mark. Vancouver had one of the largest Chinatowns—a compact, cheerful cacophony of shops and restaurants just east of downtown—in North America. As immigration ramped up, and the date approached for the 1997 return of Hong Kong to China, Vancouver's Chinese community became a focus of attention. Everyone was expecting big changes to occur.

Over the next few years, my social circle would intersect with Shiane's on infrequent occasions. Eventually, an auspicious moment arrived, when neither she nor I was seeing anyone else, and I asked her out on a date. She consented. More dates followed, and soon we grew very fond of each other.

The history of British Columbia's Chinese residents dates back many years. A few misguided nineteenth-century scholars believed that the first Chinese landed on BC's shores long before any Europeans. An author named Edward Vining tried to popularize the idea that a group of Buddhist monks, led by Hui Shen, a priest, had drifted in junks across the Pacific and visited the North American coast more than fifteen hundred years ago. Shen named the land Fusang, and his story was described in early Chinese historical texts but never substantiated.

The first Chinese visitors to definitely step ashore in BC accompanied the British fur trader John Meares from Macao to Nootka Sound in 1788. Mostly carpenters and metalworkers from southern China's Pearl River Delta, they were hired to build a base and a small ship (named the *North West America*) for the traders. The Chinese had been "generally esteemed a hardy, and industrious, as well as ingenious race of people," noted Meares in his account of the expedition. "They live on fish and rice, and, requiring but low wages, it was a matter also of economical consideration to employ them; and during the whole of the voyage there was every reason to be satisfied with their services."[1] The schooner constructed at Nootka was the first European-style vessel built on the BC coast.

It was not until the late 1850s that Chinese immigrants began to live permanently in BC. The lure was gold. Merchants came first, from the California gold diggings, followed over the next few years by several thousand miners, laundrymen, cooks and market gardeners. Many ended up going back to China. By the early 1880s, as the rush subsided, three-quarters of BC's gold miners were of Chinese origin. One thousand Chinese labourers were employed building the Cariboo Wagon Road, while five hundred more helped construct the Western Union telegraph line. They worked in fish canneries and in Vancouver Island's accident-prone coal mines. By 1885, seventeen thousand Chinese had been hired by Canadian Pacific to lay tracks for the trans-Canada railway.

Large Chinatowns sprang up in Victoria, New Westminster and Nanaimo, while smaller versions, often mining related, formed in Penticton, Cumberland, Hazelton, Boston Bar, Lillooet, Rock Creek, Quesnelle Forks, Ladner and many other places. But the most important Chinese community, of course, was in Vancouver—or Granville, as the sawmill town was known in 1884. The census that year counted 114 Chinese heads at Granville, nearly all male, nearly all working at the Hastings sawmill. That number slowly grew to about 3,500 by 1911 and 6,500 by the early 1920s. In 1923, anti-Chinese groups such as the Asiatic Exclusion League persuaded the Canadian government to pass an act that cut off any further Chinese immigration. The act was repealed in 1947, and in the 1950s, Vancouver's Chinese population more than doubled. The community Shiane was born into, in 1953, was better educated and more affluent than its predecessors. Many of its leaders were born in Canada; they spoke English and worked in professional occupations.

Members of Shiane's widespread family maintained a tight network but were also fully integrated with Vancouver's larger non-Chinese population. In many ways they enjoyed the best of two worlds. Their friends (and partners) were as likely to be white as Chinese. They kept alive their favourite Asian cultural customs (especially cuisine-related ones) but also adopted anything the city had to offer that caught their eye.

Often, when people first met Shiane and me as a couple, they would jump to the wrong conclusion; Shiane must be a recent immigrant, they thought, while I was a long-term "Canadian" of comfortably European heritage. We laughed at this because the truth was quite the opposite: I was born in Wales and had emigrated from England, with my mum and dad and younger siblings, as a nine-year-old. Shiane was a third-generation member of a pioneer Canadian family.

She had been born in BC—in the mining and smelting town of Trail, where her family had a restaurant. Her mother was born in Vancouver. It was Shiane's grandfather who had left home in Guangdong Province, travelled by boat to BC and ended up living and working in northern Alberta. He didn't, at first, understand the language or the customs of the country he'd travelled to. Over the years he and his relatives had known impoverishment and hostility. They had been discriminated against by neighbours and employers and officials. But they had survived. Many of their descendants had flourished. Now, some wanted to return to their native land—not to live, mind you, but to see where they came from, to visit relatives and to learn more about themselves. They wanted to become tourists.

The tourism-minded overseas Chinese were not the only ones in search of Asia. Inexpensive beach resorts from Turkey to Thailand were doing big business with young westerners, while the ancient temples of Vietnam and Cambodia appealed to older, culture-loving travellers. India, with its layers of history and its sophisticated cultures, had long attracted those who could bear the poverty and overcrowding. Indonesia, Japan, Sri Lanka, Myanmar and Nepal all had specialized tourist trades. Hong Kong, Bangkok and Singapore had become great gateways to the mysterious East.

Vancouver, of course, played a similar role for people headed in the other direction. For those, like Shiane and me, who grew up in Vancouver, the influx of Asian immigrants that peaked in the late 1990s (then peaked again twenty years later) was changing the city beyond all recognition. Vancouver had become China's preferred entry point to North America (though Toronto would soon grow equally popular). Earlier migrants to Canada hoped to escape poverty and political instability. Recent arrivals, however, were often able to be more selective. Affluent individuals established safe havens for their families. Asian entrepreneurs and investors purchased property as a hedge against uncertainty. With its pleasant climate, liberal politics, healthy economy and vast network of earlier migrants, Vancouver was an obvious choice for a longer stay. If they had the right qualifications, or enough money, families could immigrate to Canada permanently. Increasingly, it seemed, they had the money. In 2015, Chinese buyers spent more than $10 billion on residential real estate in Vancouver. It didn't seem to matter that the city's home prices were among the highest in the world (the average cost of a detached house in Vancouver was $1.8 million in 2015).[2]

By 2016 there were half a million people of Chinese ancestry in Greater Vancouver, about twenty percent of the total population. That number was set to almost double by 2031, according to Dan Hiebert, a University of British Columbia geography professor. Vancouver was "likely to have a social geography that is entirely new to Canadian society," Hiebert claimed in a report for Canada's immigration department. "There is no significant European city with anything like this demographic structure, nor will there be by 2031."[3] Property prices, of course, were going through the roof. Many desirable (and not-so-desirable) neighbourhoods were now dominated by Asian, mostly Chinese, families. The universities were brimming with Asian students. The satellite city of Richmond, on Vancouver's southern border, was basically a Chinese suburb—a mixed bag of restaurants and shopping malls that had taken over the title of "Chinatown" from the old Downtown Eastside community. One of the planet's most dynamic economic and racial transformations was taking place.

By 1987, the year after Shiane and I were married, enough people were flying back and forth between Vancouver and Hong Kong that Cathay Pacific, the colony's flag carrier, decided to start daily non-stop Boeing 747 service. The airline had inaugurated the route in 1983, flying twice a week, and it would eventually fly twice a day, but daily non-stop was a goal and a threshold, and it needed to be marked with a celebration. That August, I was invited to join a group of journalists for an extended weekend in Hong Kong to sample Cathay Pacific's brand of hospitality. We would fly first class (a new experience for me), stay in fine hotels, eat like we'd never eaten before and have a wonderful time. And, of course, if we felt like writing about Hong Kong and Cathay Pacific, then the company would do all it could to assist us.

I was editor of *Western Living* at the time. The magazine business was in its glory days. Technological change was racing toward us; digital publishing, digital advertising and the internet would soon transform—and destroy, some would say—our industry, but for ten years or so I was an analog "influencer." Friends used to tease me about the publication's lack of gravity, its emphasis on homes and gardens, food and fashion. We could photograph their bathrooms and kitchens any time we wanted, they joked. And wasn't it time to publish a lingerie issue? But the magazine's owners knew what they were about. The lifestyle orientation brought in advertising revenue, lots of it, which allowed us to pay good writers well to work on a wide range of topics. "As long as it's fifty percent homes and gardens," the publisher told me when I became editor, "you can do what you like with the rest." He didn't seem to be joking, so I took him at his word and ran essays, short fiction and personal journalism; profiles of local luminaries; and features on art, architecture, outdoor recreation, history and travel. Plenty of travel. A lot of perks came with the position of editor. My first trip to Asia was one of them.

The most memorable meal I had in Hong Kong that weekend was at the Bor Kee, a tiny open-air restaurant on the outlying island of Cheung Chau. We were served the simplest possible fare—gently sautéed scallops and prawns, steamed Chinese broccoli, a variety of mushrooms, rice, tea—and yet the friendly service, the unsurpassed freshness of the ingredients and the constantly changing scene in the little fishing village served to etch the afternoon on my mind.

But wait. I can remember an even better meal. We were treated to a special table d'hôte at Lai Ching Heen in the Regent, one of Hong Kong's newer and more luxurious hotels (now the InterContinental). Included in this indulgence were bird's nest soup, steamed *garrupa*, braised fresh won tons, mango pudding and a prize-winning specialty: baked, seafood-stuffed lobster tails. As I looked out across the harbour and devoured the feast with my jade and silver utensils, attended by a throng of uniformed functionaries, I thought that I had probably reached the zenith of my culinary career; dining would be all downhill from here.

And so it was, until around 11:00 p.m., when Kowloon's Temple Street came alive with a clatter of mah-jong tiles. Fortune tellers released caged finches, which selected random destiny cards from the spread in front of them and then obligingly hopped back into their bamboo prisons. There were kitchenware and sex-aid vendors, and a grinning man tried to sell me a snake. A curbside practitioner built a dental bridge for a squatting, open-mouthed patient. Street singers with three-piece string bands crooned to the passing crowds. In the middle of this poor man's nightclub, hundreds of temporary outdoor restaurants flourished. You could select your still-squirming meal-to-be from different dishes laid out on tables (perhaps the hairy brown crab would be in season, or pen shells, or whelks), then cook it yourself, fondue-style, over charcoal braziers, surrounded by the circus of the street.

I had no particular interest in Asia before that trip, no real urge to explore. But Asia was beginning to wrap itself around me, scene after scene, each one more tantalizing, more marvellous, than the last. I didn't realize it at the time, but this short, tightly controlled visit, where I saw almost nothing of everyday life and was protected from the continent's realities by a screen of affluence and ignorance, was setting in motion a spell that would bring me back, on longer and less opulent journeys, with and without friends and family members, to a dozen Asian countries over a period of thirty years.

China 1987

Shiane and I left the train in the cavernous hall of Guangzhou station and passed the scrutiny of khaki-uniformed customs officials in high-crowned caps. We realized that the week ahead would be nothing like the one we'd just spent in Hong Kong. The island colony was as slick and modern as a city in Europe. Business people and tourists from around the world thronged its shops and restaurants, its gleaming malls of tile and mirror and glass. Office and apartment towers soared. Rapid-transit systems transported visitors and residents.

The atmosphere at Guangzhou (or Canton, as it's still widely known) was very different: more like a scene from a World War I movie than a late twentieth-century border crossing. We were sternly directed to pay duty on any gifts we were bringing into the country, and to list our personal valuables, so they could be accounted for when we left. Bringing presents to one's Chinese relatives, we discovered, was an arcane ritual, full of protocol and ceremony.

Our hotel was crowded with returning overseas Chinese and their expectant kinfolk. Little clusters of people

Opposite: Catching fish with a trained cormorant on the Li River, in southern China.

waited in hallways and stairwells all around the building. My wife's task was daunting: to locate, in an alien, confusing country—using language skills she was feeling very self-conscious about—a half-sister and nephew she had never met or seen before. I'd been to Hong Kong on a brief Cathay Pacific press junket three months earlier, in August, but this was Shiane's first trip to Asia. Our whole visit to China was premised on the slim chance that a letter written from Canada by her half-brother had made its way to a tiny village in rural Guangdong Province, and that someone was available and willing to make the long trek to the city in order to meet us.

Finding no one, which was half expected, we went down to the hotel restaurant. Should we fall back on a standard tourist itinerary? Cruise the Li River? Visit the Huangmanzhai waterfalls or the dramatic karst landscapes of Guilin? We needn't have worried. Returning to our room, we were waylaid by an elderly woman in a faded maroon pantsuit and head scarf, and a beaming man in his early forties. Shiane embraced Gim Yee, her half-sister, and Tung, her nephew, and we invited them to our room. My wife discovered with relief that the smattering of village Cantonese she had learned from her mother would be sufficient for communication. Our adventure in China had begun.

Gim Yee, thirty years older than Shiane, was so excited by our visit that within minutes she was opening our suitcases to check for presents. Under normal circumstances, this eager curiosity might have resulted in a certain gruffness on my part. I knew that an open mind and heart would be required on this trip, but I hadn't expected my Western sensibilities to be tested so soon. I said nothing. Tung must have felt my alarm, for he diplomatically suggested waiting until the whole family was gathered before any gifts were distributed. My first—but far from last—moment of culture shock passed.

Tung, we learned, was working in Guangzhou on a construction site. Like tens of thousands of other men from the surrounding countryside, he had taken advantage of a recent economic liberalization and increased freedom to move about. He lived in a men's dormitory, he said, and missed his wife and two children, but he could earn far more in the city and still come home to help plant and harvest the rice. None of us could have known that the Pearl River Delta region of southern China would soon undergo an extraordinary transformation, moving from rice farming to high technology, manufacturing and foreign trade. Looking back, I realize that we were privileged to be observers at the end of an era.

The next day Shiane and I were free to wander. Tung was squeezing in a last work shift while Gim Yee took advantage of this rare city visit to shop for supplies. Guangzhou was not on a typical Western tourist itinerary; we saw few white tourists during our time there. Perhaps the great inland river port and its suburbs—home to about four million souls in 1987, a number set to triple over the next thirty years—were too congested for Western comfort. Guangzhou was the capital of Guangdong Province, one of the world's most densely populated areas, with 113 million inhabitants in 2018. It's not surprising that the region had a long history of sending workers abroad, both to earn foreign currency and to reduce pressure on land and food resources.

Guangzhou was hosting the Chinese Sixth National Games that week, and eight thousand athletes and their followers were adding their energies to the normal chaos. We were more interested in the historical and cultural links that connected the city with British Columbia, so our first goal was to find a bus to take us to Yuexiu Park, located on a hill overlooking the smoggy metropolis. Here, in a historic five-storey tower or pagoda that dated back to 1380 (though it had been destroyed and rebuilt several times over the centuries), was the Guangzhou Museum, with exhibits detailing the city's history.

A footnote to that history records that two small Royal Navy vessels limped into the mouth of the Pearl River in 1779, after exploring the west coast of North America and undertaking repairs at Nootka Sound on Vancouver Island. Both captains had died en route (Charles Clerke of tuberculosis, while James Cook, the expedition leader, was murdered in Hawaii), and the crews were anxious to rest and resupply in China—and perhaps sell for a modest profit the sea otter furs acquired in Nootka trading sessions. Little did they realize what far-reaching events they were setting in motion.

The thick, beautiful furs, many of which had been acquired for mere buttons and beads, turned out, to the sailors' astonishment, to be worth a fortune to the Chinese.

Two crewmen even stole a small boat, intending to sail back to America and buy more pelts. They were never heard from again. Better-organized entrepreneurs soon mounted larger expeditions to the Pacific Northwest, and thus began the trade in furs that would open up the European exploration of the region.

China's rulers were extremely cautious when dealing with foreigners, whom they viewed as commercial and political threats. In the 1750s they adopted a method of controlling trade, whereby all transactions for one particular region would take place at one particular location, where they could be overseen by a complicated bureaucracy of merchants and officials. This was known as the "Canton system." The last thing the government wanted was "barbarians" (as foreigners were called) wandering freely around the country influencing and contaminating people with their heretical ideas.

At the Pearl Delta, therefore, the traders' vessels were permitted to go no farther upstream than the Whampoa anchorage, a few kilometres east of Guangzhou (and now part of the city). Trade goods—mostly tea, silk and porcelain—were ferried to the ships by lighters (or "chop boats") from the Thirteen Factories, a barbarian-occupied trading enclave and warehouse district near the centre of Guangzhou. The factories were destroyed by fire on several occasions, then rebuilt on nearby Shamian Island, now a peaceful neighbourhood of parks, restaurants, hotels, European-style buildings and tree-lined pedestrian avenues. Shamian once served as the consulate precinct and still maintains a historic colonial atmosphere. It was here that we found ourselves at the end of a busy day of sightseeing.

At five thirty the next morning, Gim Yee brought us sticky rice dumplings with chicken wrapped in lotus leaves, which we ate while drinking tea. Tung had helped us hire a minibus and driver, and today he would guide us on an eighteen-hour expedition into the countryside. We travelled on the main road south to Jiangmen, across the flat, fertile deltas of the Pearl (Zhu) and Xi Rivers. In our smart red minibus, we strained to pass a slow-moving throng of bicycles, scooters, buses, trucks and trailers. It's amazing what a Chinese farmer can fit on a motorcycle: six pigs, a dozen geese, two dozen chickens, great baskets of vegetables, his family.

At the shore of the Xi's main stem, a motley flotilla of ferries plied frantically back and forth, slapping their landing ramps down on the riverbank wherever there was space. The great bridge that crosses there now was still under construction. (A dozen other large bridges would soon be built to connect the Pearl Delta's numerous islands and improve their economic potential.) A dense layer of grey fog hugged the water, making the channel look as wide as the ocean. Passing through this swirling veil seemed to separate us from the known world.

Midmorning we reached the city of Taishan (Toisan), where we were greeted by a white banner stretched across the road. "Welcome to Toisan, Home of the Overseas Chinese," it said, in English and Chinese. The sign wasn't entirely correct;

overseas Chinese came from many parts of the country. But Taishan was certainly a major source for the tens of thousands of labourers who emigrated to North America from the Pearl Delta during the second half of the nineteenth century. Shiane's paternal grandfather was one of them.

Taishan felt strange to me, divided. The division was not just between those whose relatives had gone to "Gold Mountain," as North America was popularly known, and those whose relatives had stayed in China. No, everyone in Taishan had an ancestor who had made the journey. Five hundred thousand Chinese Americans are estimated to be of Taishanese descent. The division was between the families that had benefited, whose forebears had flourished in the New World and sent back money, and the ones whose grandfathers and great-uncles were never seen or heard from again.

Taishan was a study in contrasts: fine houses, private schools and hospitals stood beside rundown shops and crumbling apartment blocks. Many welcoming faces hailed our little entourage (the expensive rented minibus marked us as overseas visitors), but I saw bitterness and envy also. Shiane's grandfather had prospered in Gold Mountain, enough to return as a rich man and lord it over his home village, but for every success story there were a dozen tales of woe, a hundred mysterious absences. For most Chinese immigrants, Gold Mountain was a place of suffering and tragedy, where loneliness, discrimination and abuse were routine.

We stopped at Taishan's best restaurant, where I was to host a celebratory lunch. A happy crowd of relatives and friends awaited, and as lunch proceeded, the number of guests began to expand alarmingly. Gim Yee was beckoning acquaintances to join us off the street, and I began to worry about the size of the impending bill. But lunch in rural China—even for fifty—was then still not expensive. As we left the restaurant, two dozen other people showed up, downcast at having missed the meal. Gim Yee screeched at them for their lamentable timing.

As our expanded cavalcade headed into the countryside toward Gim Yee's village, I struggled to see her side of the picture. Her father had followed his father to North America, where he had enjoyed a long life, earning and losing, by Chinese standards, several fortunes. He had arranged for Gim Yee's two brothers to emigrate to Canada, where they now lived comfortable lives. But she was still stuck here, a rural peasant. She had suffered during the Communist Revolution; she had suffered during the Cultural Revolution. The least we could do was redress the balance with gifts.

Gim Yee's house was one of the largest in the village, a one-storey, three-room affair under a flat roof. The open central area was for living. The family slept in one wing, while the pigs, separated by a brick wall, occupied the other. We passed out the long-awaited presents: money and clothing brought from Canada, sweets and cigarettes from Hong Kong, biscuits and booze from Guangzhou. Gim Yee proudly showed us the colour television—a Toshiba, mind you, not a Chinese-made job—that had been bought the previous year, along with a Singer sewing machine, by Shiane's half-brother.

The silent television, watched by a group of kids and some chickens in case it should miraculously come to life, sat in a special cabinet at the heart of the living room. This was so it could be locked up—the only object in the entire village, we were told, valuable enough to rate such treatment. Private property had infiltrated the village's communal lifestyle: the television was a bomb in disguise, an ideological Trojan Horse from the developed world. I could imagine this shining status symbol gradually insinuating itself into the community like a slow-release capsule, then changing it forever.

After tea, we continued our tour, which didn't take long. We greeted most of the hamlet's hundred or so inhabitants, smiling and shaking hands furiously. We inspected a number of friendly pigs. On the roof of the house, where rice would later be spread to dry, family photographs were taken. The watching neighbours giggled benevolently, especially when I set my camera on the wall and used the self-timer to include myself in the picture. After the automatic click, a collective exhalation could be heard.

The next stop on our journey was a nearby town, the birthplace of my wife's grandfather. In the early twentieth century, this pioneering migrant had established a laundry in Edson, a small Albertan town, and made enough money to return home and build a solid, granite, two-storey house with decorative stone trim around the windows and roof. He became a prominent landowner, a bad choice for the revolution years. After he died in 1951, his house was "liberated," and distant cousins managed to get the place assigned to them as living quarters. The interior was gloomy and dusty; the current occupants appeared to be camping in the dilapidated shell. The remains of faded, hand-painted wall murals still overlooked the scene, and the chipped wooden balustrades and stair railings were of delicate lathework. Gim Yee produced a wizened little man who was reputed to be more than one hundred years old and a friend of Shiane's grandfather. Startled, perhaps, by the sudden attention, he kept any revelations he may have had to himself.

Finally, it was time to leave. We still had to locate Ying, the youngest sister of Shiane's mother, who lived in a different district and whose name and village had been written out for us on a scrap of paper. For two hours we drove hither and thither over the Pearl Delta, having numerous roadside consultations with bystanders. With the help of Tung, who was coming back to Guangzhou with us, and our stalwart, patient driver, we eventually began to close in on the elusive destination. The last few kilometres took us over dirt tracks through rice paddies and vegetable plots. We constantly had to stop while farmers moved their produce and tools aside and let us pass.

Late in the afternoon we reached Ying's village. Shiane's aunt was another of those who had been left behind while the rest of her family had managed to move to the promised land. Ying had also received a letter saying that we would try to visit her, and she met Shiane with both joy and sadness, for my wife's mother had died earlier that year, and Ying would never again meet the older sister from whom she had been separated in childhood.

Ying's husband and I left the two women to mourn together while he showed me the sights: the fabulously clean communal bathroom facility with its octagonal arrangement of squat toilets; the orange orchards for which the area was famous. Through sign language and gesture he let me know that Ying had a serious illness: a rare type of cancer, we later found out. I tried to convey to him my condolences and tell him that Shiane also had health problems. About a year before, only six months after we married, she had been diagnosed with colon cancer and had undergone major surgery. Her treatment, we were told, was successful, but we knew that, at thirty-three, she was young to have this kind of illness. It did not bode well for her long-term future. After the surgery, a natural sense of urgency came over Shiane. She became a student again, a searcher. Her quest was for practical knowledge, certainly, to increase her chances of survival, but also for self-awareness. It was this search that had brought us to China. I had worried that such travel would be too hard on her, so soon after her operation, but she was determined to see, for the first time, the world of her ancestors.

As Ying prepared to serve us tea before the long journey back to the city, I had a small epiphany. To my great surprise, on the wall above the household shrine, I found a photo of my parents, my wife and me: a picture from our wedding the year before. So far from home, in such an improbable location, the unexpected image exploded in my psyche; the vast differences between us of place and race, of wealth and social condition, collapsed. Here we all were, under the same bright sky, doing the best we could. Deep in my heart, I felt truly connected to Shiane's relatives for the first time. They were my kin also. Unlikely as it might seem at first glance, we were one.[4]

Photo Gallery

Shiane and Gim Yee outside home built by Shiane's grandfather, Guangdong Province.

Shiane and Gim Yee with elderly family friend.

Rooftop view from Gim Yee's village in rural Guangdong Province, China.

Floating village at Ayothaya, Thailand.

The enormous Buddha figures at Polonnaruwa, Sri Lanka, are carved from a single mass of granite.

Stupa decoration detail, Bangkok, Thailand.

Fish vendor at a market in Goa.

Mahabalipuram, India. A girl decorates the entrance to her family home with a welcoming design.

Excursion vessel skipper contemplates entering Sipja Donggul (the Cross-Shaped Cave) on the South Korean coast.

Headquarters of the Cao Dai sect at Tây Ninh in southern Vietnam. Sect members venerate Victor Hugo and Sun Yat-sen among other prophets.

Hanoi sidewalk sculptor specializes in images of Vietnam's Ho Chi Minh.

On a day trip to Tam Coc a woman poles visitors through the dramatic landscapes of Vietnam's Three Gorges.

A basket vendor eyes a potential customer in Hanoi's Old Quarter, Vietnam.

Laos 1991

Dawn was breaking as the overnight train from Bangkok arrived at the town of Nong Khai. The inevitable scrum of tuk-tuks—small three-wheeled taxis, half motorcycle, half buggy—vied for the attention of the passengers, who were few, for this was not a tourist route. At the river landing where you crossed the great Mekong and entered the Lao People's Democratic Republic, the customs office was still closed. A nearby row of open-air restaurants teetered delicately over the riverbank. I waited there, sleepy and stiff, with a cup of instant coffee, and watched a fisherman lay his nets. From a distance, silhouetted against the brightening sky, he appeared to dance, his arms making graceful, elaborate movements as he cleaned and let out a long filament my eyes could not detect.

It was early November, and the water level was high. Even here, at least fifteen hundred kilometres from its mouth in Vietnam, the brown, muddy river was almost two kilometres wide. In dry season huge mud flats would emerge; before they disappeared with the rising flood, local farmers on both sides would quickly harvest a crop of vegetables. The river formed much of Thailand's long border with Laos; Nong Khai, where a fleet of tiny wooden ferries plied back and forth all day, was one of the few legal crossing points. After customs stamped an exit date in your passport, you had to clamber down a steep set of steps to the water and cautiously board a boat.

Near here, with financial help from Australia, the first vehicular bridge was being constructed over the Mekong, and this border station would soon be replaced by a more up-to-date one. But that morning, out in the middle of the river, equal measures of fear and anticipation gripped me and focused my attention. I was in no man's land, between the tourist trails of Thailand and the mystery of Laos. Ahead was unknown territory.

Few people visited landlocked, mountainous Laos in the early 1990s. Once the heartland of Lan Xang, "kingdom of one million elephants"—a great fourteenth-century empire whose constantly shifting borders covered parts of China, Cambodia, Burma (now Myanmar), Thailand and Vietnam—Laos was now one of the world's poorest nations. Restrictions on foreign visitors and investment had recently been loosened by its rigid but financially desperate government. But unlike Myanmar and Cambodia, where, in 1991, tourists had to fly in with an organized group, Laos grudgingly let you cross the border on foot and visit certain areas as an independent traveller.

My goal was to get to Luang Prabang, the ancient royal capital of Laos, about 250 kilometres to the north. Intriguing rumours kept drifting my way: that it was Asia's last, untouched Shangri-La; that few westerners had seen its exotic monuments; that the strange and unforeseen could occur there—as it had to a friend of mine, travelling on United Nations business, who found himself sharing his hotel breakfast table with a Canadian tourist named Pierre Elliott Trudeau. The fluid, musical name of Luang Prabang had become my travel mantra.

In truth, I was also looking for a quiet place to assuage my grief. My wife, Shiane, had died that spring after almost five years of battling cancer. She was only thirty-seven, and much loved. Family and friends had created a hospice for her, a pleasant, private apartment where she was able to die peacefully, with dignity and grace. The process of looking after her had had a powerful effect on us, and we were devastated by her death. I don't know what had possessed me to think that travelling around Southeast Asia would help me get over my loss. I guess I'd felt that I was ready to resume a normal life. But I was wrong. It was too soon. I was travelling like a ghost, unable to connect or engage, a prisoner of my delusions.

After being pushed through Lao customs by an urgent crowd, I first had to get to Vientiane, twenty kilometres away. Public transportation seemed non-existent. Finally, after visiting a compound where an English-teaching program operated, I reached the city in a United Nations pickup truck, courtesy of a Canadian international development worker I'd met at the border. Most of the westerners I met in Laos were international development workers.

With a population, in 1991, of three hundred thousand

or so, Vientiane, on a fertile flood plain of the Mekong, was the capital and by far the largest city of Laos. Its stately, tree-lined avenues—some culminating in odd bits of ostentation, like a triumphal, arched independence monument, which you could climb for the view—were evidently designed for a more glorious future than the one that had arrived. Other streets were flanked by rundown colonial buildings erected by the French, who had made Laos part of Indochina in 1893, two chaotic centuries after the collapse of the Lan Xang empire.

Laos gained independence in 1953, and to all appearances, it could still have been 1953 in Vientiane. This time lock was not difficult to explain. For more than two decades after winning its freedom, Laos had become a battleground for Communist guerrillas, disaffected army officers and followers of the US-backed royal family. And since the Pathet Lao had taken over in 1975, the country had suffered a lengthy period of heavy-handed Communist rule. The only recent construction I saw in 1991 was the fine new Morning Market, which was stocked with plenty of Thai goods.

After checking into a hotel, I set out to seek transport to Luang Prabang. Theoretically, you could get there from Vientiane by bus, on a winding dirt road through the mountains, or on a three-day riverboat trip, as both cities were on the Mekong. Tourists, however, had to fly: travel by land was too dangerous. Theoretically, again, you could wander over to Lao Aviation and buy a return ticket for a very reasonable price, but, for tourists, this was not allowed either. You had to deal with the same travel agency that arranged your entry into the country. Thus, over tea in a little hotel office, I conducted the first in a series of delicate negotiations with the estimable Mr. Bounheng, cheerful proprietor of the Thatluang Tour Company.

How many of me were there? Just one? Tsk, tsk. The tourism ministry did not like to issue a travel permit for just one person. Much cheaper to join a group. All right, I said, figuring that I could ditch the group later and do my own thing. Unfortunately, there were no groups at the moment. Would I like to buy a complete package tour? I looked at the prices. They were more than I wanted to pay. All I needed was the travel permit and the air ticket. Mr. Bounheng put his fingers together and pursed his lips. I could check with him tomorrow, but ... he shook his head and looked exceedingly doubtful.

Friends in Bangkok had warned me that travel arrangements were haphazard in Laos. I was not to be disappointed if I couldn't reach Luang Prabang. Sometimes tourists could go there; sometimes they couldn't. Sometimes the plane flew; sometimes it didn't. Sometimes two planes flew. So that night, to disguise the disappointment I was not supposed to feel, I ate at the Nam Phou, one of several good restaurants in town where faint echoes of the French regime could still be found.

I had a Pernod, vegetable soup, filet mignon and marvellous Laotian café au lait. The crusty bread rolls were fresh and warm, the service friendly and attentive. Expats and diplomats nattered at the bar. The bill came to the equivalent of about ten dollars. I proffered a five-hundred-baht Thai banknote in payment and received two hundred baht, one hundred Laotian kip and a US dollar in change. I felt better. Worldly, even, ready for anything—including the punishing imitation of rock 'n' roll that a live Lao band and female singer were performing back at my hotel.

The next day I had another go at Mr. Bounheng. Why did I wish to procure my own hotel and meals and arrange my own side trips? Why did I wish to stay in an inexpensive hotel? I was a disappointment to Mr. Bounheng. And also, perhaps, for the Laotian economy. But when ultimately persuaded that it was the bare bones or nothing, the all-important travel permit was issued, and the flight, which had by then mysteriously doubled in price, booked.

After this small victory I looked for a likely means of touring the city. On the streets there were lots of shiny new Honda scooters, but most people were still pedalling. I rented a bicycle and joined them. I visited the sights: Phra Kaew, a museum and former temple that once housed the Emerald Buddha (now in Bangkok and Thailand's most revered religious image); and That Luang, a sixteenth-century stupa destroyed and rebuilt several times over the years, which had become a potent focal point of Lao nationalism. There were few other tourists, which was fine with me. After a month in Thailand—a wonderful, inexpensive place and thus chockablock with visitors, particularly young people with small budgets and large backpacks—I had been yearning to get away from the crowds.

That night I walked along the riverbank. Across the water the lights of Thailand twinkled. Young men practised their English by calling out soft greetings as they bicycled by. Through the dusty air you could smell the oranges at the roadside stalls. I stumbled across a Buddhist ceremony, with actors in bright antique costumes singing and chasing one another to the tormenting beat of an amplified cymbal. Dozens of spellbound children watched. Tall candles illuminated a nearby altar where people were lighting incense and leaving colourful fabric and paper offerings. Then a bonfire was started and all the pretty offerings thrown on it.

At a waterfront restaurant, where locals and foreigners were noisily drinking the excellent Laotian beer, I stopped and had a celebratory meal. The menu, partly in French, listed soup with vegetables and prawns. I ordered it. The waitress seemed startled. She made voluptuous motions with her hands and I nodded yes. Soon a whole Mekong catfish was sitting in front of me in a fish-shaped saucepan set over a burner. A dark sauce with sliced yellow vegetables bubbled around it. Some raw green stuff that looked like watercress was piled on top. I received a spoon and a small soup bowl. A larger bowl of sauce appeared.

I stared at the food. But I ordered fish soup, I kept thinking. How am I supposed to eat this? The waitress, perhaps responding to the tip I'd left earlier as I sat drinking a beer, took pity on my helplessness and showed me how to cut the fish up, spoon it into the little bowl along with the broth and vegetables and then replace the sauce from the larger bowl. The green stuff melted down into the broth. The fish had been deep-fried first; the skin was crinkly and delicious, the flesh white and solid, with few bones. I don't know what happened to the prawns.

Any apprehensions I might have had about flying in Laos were immediately doubled at Vientiane's domestic airport by the appearance of a fellow passenger wearing a white T-shirt with DEATH printed on it. I was pathetically grateful when she took a different flight. Our aircraft, a Chinese-built Y7, was like an oven, unbearable. As soon as we took off, alarming clouds of white smoke began to seep into the cabin: air conditioning, communist-style. Nobody took the slightest notice.

We flew low, over the serene and beautiful Laotian countryside, all rice paddies and meandering streams. On one Mekong tributary we could see Nam Ngum, the country's only dam (and a significant foreign exchange earner, exporting surplus electricity to Thailand), with a big reservoir behind it. Then, for forty-five uninterrupted minutes, we were above rugged green mountains, with one thin, red dirt road snaking through them.

The residents of this picturesque scene were why it was too dangerous for tourists to travel by land. Here, in little thatched villages on bamboo stilts, connected only by footpaths and surrounded by the slash-and-burn evidence of their subsistence agriculture, lived the hill-tribe people—Hmong, Mien, Tai, Akha and others—who not so long ago produced much of the world's opium. They still grew opium here.

The tribes comprised half the country's population (the other half, the dominant Lao ethnic group, who migrated from southwestern China and created the kingdom of Lan Xang, lived in the fertile, rice-growing river valleys). Most hill people had arrived from Burma, China and Tibet centuries after the Lao.

Enmity had long existed between certain hill tribes and the Communist guerrillas, now in power. Arming friendly tribesmen in Laos had kept the CIA busy during the Vietnam War, accounting for many of the legendary Air America flights. Even in 1991 the government did not completely control the country's remoter regions. And considering the terrain one could see from the airplane, one might be forgiven for thinking that most of Laos qualified as a remoter region. Bandits flourished out there. People disappeared.

Soon we swooped down from the mountains and followed the broad, muddy course of the Mekong. At its junction with another river, the Nam Khan, a cluster of white and golden spires broke through the dark forest canopy and gradually revealed itself as a town of perhaps thirty thousand people: Luang Prabang. Its remote setting was lush and hilly, covered with ebony trees and coconut palms. Compared with the lowland cauldron of Vientiane, the air was fresh and cool. If Vientiane had seemed stuck in the 1950s, then here the calendar had slipped away altogether. This was old Asia: a timeless dimension of dust and bicycles and long stares.

Luang Prabang was the country's religious and cultural centre, and there seemed to be an antique Buddhist monastery (wat) on every corner. Hundreds of saffron-robed monks (and boys, who were educated at the temples) roamed the streets carrying black umbrellas. The most important of the more than thirty wats—sixteenth-century Xieng Thong and the newer Mai Suwannaphumaham—were beside the river, as was the royal palace. Religious myths and legends were retold on the pagoda walls, in exquisite mosaics of coloured glass. Wooden doors and gables were elaborately carved. Old stone steps led down to the water, where ornate barges had once docked in order to transport high-ranking monks and royalty.

Never conquered or damaged, this town had been royal since the eleventh century. Originally called Muong Swa, it had alternated with Vientiane as the capital of Lan Xang, and when the empire fell, it continued as capital of the smaller kingdom of Luang Prabang. When Laos came into being, the kings of Luang Prabang became the kings of Laos. When King Sisavang Vatthana was forced to give up the throne in 1975, 622 years of continuous recorded monarchy ended.

The royal palace had been turned into a museum. Inside, despite the presence of several thirty-centimetre-high Buddhas of solid gold, the only staff in view were three women reclining languidly on the gleaming hardwood floors of the entrance hall. A few years ago, I'd been told, someone took advantage of the innocent Laotian attitude toward tourism and stole several religious icons from Luang Prabang; officials were so outraged that for a time they closed the entire country's borders to foreign visitors.

In front of the palace was a regal, palm-lined promenade, down which processions of royal elephants used to march in New Year celebrations, while caged birds and animals were released to garner spiritual merit for the royal family. No longer, of course. King Vatthana, implicated in a coup two years after abdicating, was sent to a "re-education" camp in the rural north, where he is believed to have died.

I think I was the only independent traveller in Luang Prabang that week. The delight I felt at being there, however, was tinged with guilt. Here was one of those increasingly rare places that had neither been overexposed to Western culture nor succumbed to materialism. And here was I, the thin edge of the wedge (indeed, tourism in Laos would multiply by a factor of twenty between 1990 and 2010). Would my few reluctant tourist dollars bring hospitals and schools, a better life? Would the inevitable changes that my presence foreshadowed be worth the price? The vitality and freshness I found were hard to reconcile with the poverty and backwardness. A debate over the morality of tourism began to preoccupy my thoughts. And with it came an image of myself, as if from the distant past: colonialist, corrupter of innocence. My mind put it away as quickly as the flick of a snake's tongue.

"Why do you come here?" asked Surith, the manager of my hotel (the Rama, ten dollars a night, cold water and fan). It was a good question and deserved a thoughtful answer.

I tried to tell him about the inner impulses that had propelled me to Laos. He shook his head slightly and looked away. Who knows what he was thinking? Still, he spent hours on the hotel veranda with me, sharpening his English, while servers brought us glasses of Chinese tea and an endless stream of bicycles passed by.

One day a strange thing happened. I pulled the drawer of the desk in my room out further than usual and noticed some paper at the back. I looked more closely. It was money, a thick wad of Laotian kip. I counted it, about fifty dollars' worth: a small fortune in this country, the equivalent of several weeks' pay. What should I do? Leave it where it was? Show it to the manager? I decided on the latter, but when I went downstairs nobody was around. Later, I thought.

I jumped on my rented bicycle and rode out of town, where the streets soon became dirt tracks and the friendly people dirt poor. There were butterflies everywhere. Women were weaving richly patterned traditional cloth on hand looms. Brave youngsters tested my giant, white, hairy presence by calling out "*sawadee*," and laughing mothers stopped to show me to stunned toddlers. A novice monk asked that I photograph him with his friends and send him a picture; he proudly wrote out his address in English.

Two boys beckoned to me and pointed at a pile of rocks. All I could see was a pile of rocks. They pointed again, and I drew closer, closer, until I realized that I was about fifteen centimetres away from the largest spider I'd ever encountered, a hairy brown tarantula as big as my outstretched hand, perfectly hidden against its earthy background. Eight black eyes regarded me with alarm. I knew the tarantulas here were harmless, but my head jerked back involuntarily in sudden horror. The boys laughed.

The money in my hotel room preyed on my mind. It was bizarre. How could a Laotian lose so much loot? Had someone been murdered? Was it a trick or a trap? Perhaps it was the custom here, with foreign currency inconvenient to change, to leave some local stuff for guests. You just settled up when you left. Nah, that was ridiculous. Were the Laotian secret police testing me to see if I was a fit candidate for an urgent mission? If I turned the money in, would the manager pocket it and dine out for the rest of his life on stupid-tourist stories?

Rather than cash another traveller's cheque, I started spending the money as mine ran out. I hired a boat to go up the river to the sacred Tham Ting cave lined with carved Buddhas. I climbed Phousi Hill for its fine view; at the top a decayed piece of field artillery pointed at the airport while a weathered sign forbade photography. I wrote letters that never arrived at their destinations (although the post office did provide pots of glue for affixing the ungummed Laotian stamps). As the banknotes in my room grew fewer, I replaced them with their equivalent in Thai bills. Someone else could resolve my dilemma.

One day I visited a pot-making village, whose trademark, on the shoulder of each pot, was a small decorative lizard. Nobody was working the day I went because a villager had died. The dead man's relatives invited me into his bamboo hut and gave me tea. The dead man himself rested beside us in his coffin, which was wrapped in coloured foil like a giant Christmas present. On the way back I was surprised to see other actual tourists, rattling around in an air-conditioned bus. They were French, a tour group staying at the Mitaphab, the "good" hotel, where a sign posted by the Red Cross pleaded with guests to donate spare medical supplies to the local hospital.

In the evenings, I talked to Surith ("People in Laos very honest; we have no crime here," he told me) and to the energetic development workers, all poorly paid volunteers, also staying at the Rama. Roberta, a Canadian, worked for UNICEF with a troupe of Lao musicians and puppeteers, presenting folk dramas to outlying villages about the dangers of childhood dysentery. Michael, an Australian archaeologist, was excavating an old temple up the river. Terry, an English aquaculture expert, was studying the fish of the Mekong. Half the river's nine hundred species had not even been scientifically described, he guessed, including an endangered giant catfish that could reach a length of three metres and a weight of three hundred kilograms. Terry spent his spare time on the waterfront, questioning fishermen and poking around in their catch baskets.

At night Luang Prabang was black, the streets unlit, the people indoors. Power failures were frequent. Next to the Rama was a sort of club with an astonishingly bad band and a large number of teenaged girls whom you could dance with, and more, I'd heard, if you paid them. Heinekens were a buck each. Across the street you could eat broad rice noodles and duck and vegetables and drink tea for about the same price.

On my last night I went to Wat Phra Bat Tai, built right on the riverbank around its Buddha's footprint. A patient dog waited for me to unlatch the gate. The monastery, all towers and spires, was spooky by twilight. Nocturnal animals, lizards perhaps, rustled in the fallen leaves. Crickets croaked, and a gigantic moth glanced off my shirt. The monks were busy with their evening prayers.

Down a set of broken steps I stopped and leaned against a rail. Why had I come to this forgotten country? My grief remained unassuaged, but that didn't seem important anymore. My sorrow would pass ... or not. I sighed. It was time to rejoin the world. The sun set quickly in tangerine splendour. A crescent moon rose over the swirling, chuckling river. Soon, for a town of thirty thousand, the darkness was eerie; I could see only two or three points of light along the entire shoreline. Under the bright stars a huge Buddha loomed through the trees, protective but alien. The chanting of the monks, unchanged for centuries, went on and on.

Sri Lanka 1993

At Colombo's Katunayake Airport we were asked to pose for a photograph with our tourist board hosts. There was sufficient interest, apparently, in the fact that my father was returning to Sri Lanka more than half a century after his first visit, for a photographer to have been dispatched the thirty or so kilometres from Colombo. He was a short, smiling fellow wearing a sarong and the traditional white Muslim cap that identified him as a hajji, one who has made the pilgrimage to Mecca.

"Are you the son?" he asked me as he arranged us in a row. I gave him an incredulous glance, but he seemed serious. Either Pa had aged exceedingly well or I hadn't. I thought back to the hotel in Singapore, where the pretty receptionist had looked at our names on the check-in form, then at our faces, and smiled. "You must be brothers," she'd said sweetly. Perhaps she wasn't joking. Let's just assume that our photographer was zealous, double-checking his facts with care. Anyway, at seventy-eight my father was as active and curious as many people half his age, and raring to check out his old haunts.

Opposite: At the Pinnawala Elephant Orphanage, Sri Lanka.

In due course, our photo would appear under "local news" in the *Observer*, the oldest English newspaper in southern Asia, founded in 1834. There, sandwiched between a picture of a cabinet minister inaugurating a rural electrification scheme and a report of a cholera outbreak in the northern city of Jaffna, a caption tried to explain why we were on the island.

"Jack David Scott," it began, "second from right, author of three books ... lived in Sri Lanka fifty years ago during World War II." The caption, generous but inaccurate, went on to ascribe my own writing credentials to my father also. I loomed gormlessly in the background, without apparent purpose. We both looked a bit dishevelled and stunned, as if we could hardly believe we were here. This at least was true.

In 1940, my father finished officer's training in England and was sent "east." He had elected to join the Royal Artillery, but the most coveted postings—to units in Malaya—were taken by the time *S* was reached on the personnel lists, and he ended up in what is now Pakistan's Khyber Pakhtunkhwa province (formerly the North-West Frontier Province). In 1940, it was part of India.

Japan's entry into the war changed everything. After the surprise attack on Pearl Harbor in December 1941, Japanese forces raced down the Malay Peninsula (wiping out the British artillery garrisons), sank the Royal Navy's two most important warships in the region and, in February 1942, took Singapore. Australia was now at risk, and the

Allies feared a Japanese thrust across the Bay of Bengal at India and Ceylon. In April 1942, Japanese planes did indeed bomb several southern Asian ports, including Colombo, Ceylon's capital and main city, and sank a number of ships.

Pa, meanwhile, after a stint at the staff college at Quetta, had been posted to the newly formed Twentieth Indian Division. Its first mission was to entrain for Ceylon, where it was to relieve a battle-scarred Australian division diverted in haste to the island's defence while sailing home from North Africa. The Australian government, understandably, was eager for the return of its soldiers. As it happened, the Japanese decided to advance on India overland via Burma, and Ceylon was never in serious danger. But the Allies were not to know this, and so, in the early summer of 1942, my father's six-thousand-man division, raw as a crate of bright green mangoes, found itself rolling through southern India en route to the pilgrimage centre and port of Rameswaram.

A captain by this time, Pa looked after supplies and ammunition for the divisional artillery regiments, which sported thirty-two 4.5-inch field howitzers. At Rameswaram, a train ferry ran to Talaimannar in Ceylon, across the Palk Strait (the service was cancelled in 1985 because of Tamil terrorist activity). For the final leg of the journey, everything had to be unloaded from the Indian trains and reloaded onto Ceylonese trains, which used a different-gauge rail. No one had any idea what was ahead of them. For my father, not yet twenty-seven, Ceylon was a strange and exotic adventure.

Fifty-odd years later, our journey to Colombo would be somewhat different. We were in a comfortable van, accompanied by Vernon, our delightful host from the Ceylon Tourist Board—who explained that his organization had changed its name from Sri Lanka Tourist Board back to the original "because no one knew who we were"—and Ramachandra, our Tamil driver. They would be our constant companions for the next two weeks.

The two-lane road from airport to city was jammed with trucks and three-wheelers. But some things, perhaps, hadn't changed much: there were few street lights, and in the sultry darkness we passed bullock-powered carts, young women walking hand in hand and small groups of cigarette-smoking men clustered around the insignificant flames of portable food stalls.

And here was another feature of Sri Lanka that had remained as it was in 1943, when Pa last saw it: the Galle Face Hotel, where we were to stay in Colombo. The hotel remained much as it was in 1864, in fact—oceanside, facing the long promenade of the Galle Face Green, now brown and eroded from use. The brightest stars had twinkled here when the hotel was the best in town: Indira Gandhi and Ursula Andress, George Bernard Shaw and Yuri Gagarin. There was a list beside the entrance, with quotes. "Time is experienced in a different way," the queen of Denmark claimed, while according to the Aga Khan, "happiness is the GFH."

Later, seated on the terrace with a drink, Pa raked through his memories and found that nothing was as he recollected. In 1943, the carpets and the furniture were new; the foyers and public rooms pulsated with energy and anticipation. This was the place to be in Ceylon; the hotel was thronged with the affluent and powerful: planters, government officials, army brass, visiting dignitaries and their satellites.

Now the musty, cavernous hallways echoed. The handful of German and Italian tourists were lost in the vast spaces. The elderly staff, who carried themselves with enormous dignity, outnumbered the guests. Like the hotel, they had seen better days. Eccentricities had crept in: "GFH admires your decision not to smoke," one sign proclaimed; another, at the top of the stairs, said, "Please walk down. It's good for you."

We were given enormous adjacent suites—the Royal Thai and the Royal Commonwealth—for two nights, the only period in three weeks of travelling together that we would not be sharing a hotel room. I hadn't spent this much time in such close quarters with my father in years. We had gone on a journey together once before, to the Yucatán, but that was in 1980. I had been thirty-three. I seem to remember that we got on each other's nerves a little, that I found it difficult to appreciate him just the way he was. In retrospect, I think my real difficulty was in seeing how alike we were—another way of saying that it was myself I couldn't accept, not him. Fathers and sons are such mirrors for each other. Cherishing all one might see there—weak and strong, admirable and irritating—is a longer journey than the one we were on today.

And even this journey, which had taken much time and tribulation to put together, felt like a quest of some sort. But what sort? I didn't think it was a Hollywood fantasy we were living out. My father was revisiting a fundamental, deeply remembered scene from his youth, when everything was still possible. I was just along for the ride, hoping to get to know him—and thus, of course, myself—better.

Before leaving Colombo, we had a celebrity to visit and respects to pay. And so, at noon precisely, we found ourselves on a side street, pushing the buzzer at Leslie's House, a leafy compound belonging to the nation's most famous foreign resident. Pa had obtained this person's address and written to him from Canada, asking if he would see us.

Our quarry—a notoriously busy writer and futurist, author of more than fifty books—was noncommittal, but at least he sent back a form letter, explaining that he was suffering from post-polio syndrome and was limiting his workday to ten hours. Handwritten across the bottom was a note: "Phone me when you arrive." Pa, an author himself and a retired lawyer, phoned, negotiated and persuaded. Arthur C. Clarke had kindly agreed to grant us ten minutes. At noon, precisely.

Manil, his secretary, ushered us upstairs, past a display cabinet of mementoes from *2001: A Space Odyssey* and other astronautic encounters, into an office where three assistants were sitting at computers, then into a large, book-lined study. At one end, there was a sofa and armchair arrangement; at the other, Arthur C. himself, working furiously to finish *The Snows of Olympus: A Garden on Mars*, forthcoming that year from Gollancz.

On closer inspection we discovered that Clarke, while indeed hard at it, had reached the fun part of this particular project. The text was complete; all that remained was for him to enhance a series of close-up digital satellite images of Mars, using a program from a California company called Virtual Reality Laboratories. The software had him totally engrossed. He invited us behind his desk; a barren, volcanic landscape filled the big screen of his Compaq. Deftly manipulating his mouse, he added different types of vegetation and a small lake, changing colour, texture and shading instantly to suit his whim.

"Terraforming," I said, brightly, no stranger to *Star Trek*.

"Exactly," replied Clarke, with a smile.

Clarke had lived in Sri Lanka, on and off, since 1956, when he was drawn to the island through his fascination with diving (which, in turn, he had become interested in as a result of trying to experience the weightlessness of space travel). His explorations of Sri Lanka's tropical reefs, especially the Great Basses off the south coast, where he and his partner Mike Wilson discovered the wreck of an eighteenth-century Dutch treasure ship, had been documented in half a dozen books.

Although Clarke now lived in Colombo, his heart, he claimed, longed for a gorgeous arc of palm-treed beach lining Unawatuna Bay, where he'd spent many of his younger days. He described his island life in *The View from Serendip*, a collection of miscellaneous writings containing "fragments of an equatorial autobiography." (Serendip was an ancient name for Sri Lanka.)

Clarke also set one of his science-fiction novels, *The Fountains of Paradise*, in Taprobane (another old name for Sri Lanka). The story concerned the construction of a space elevator, which the protagonist is determined to erect on the summit of Sri Pada, or Adam's Peak, a famous temple and pilgrimage site. Much of the action occurred at the ancient fortress and landmark of Sigiriya, one of Clarke's favourite places. He handed us a slide viewer with a shot of the sheer-walled monolith and urged us to visit it. We felt obliged to follow his advice. Politeness demanded it.

Sitting at his keyboard in a sarong, with a videophone placed prominently on his desk (the first one I'd seen—and in Sri Lanka of all places), the white-haired, seventy-six-year-old Clarke, owlish in thick glasses, still put in a full day of work, despite the discomfort of a recent abdominal operation. He showed us a list of current projects: TV pilots (one by Steven Spielberg), a twenty-six-part YTV series, an "aquabiography," a collection of essays, live interviews (via videophone, of course), the convocation address at Sri Lanka's University of Moratuwa, home to the Arthur C. Clarke Centre. Three of his books—*The Hammer of God, The Fountains of Paradise* and *Childhood's End*—had been optioned for movies, while Mike Oldfield wanted to compose a musical suite based on *The Songs of Distant Earth*.

We'd had almost half an hour with Clarke, and it was time to go. As we left, I asked him whether he went off-island very often. He paused a second and then shook his head. "I hope never to leave Sri Lanka again," he said, without a trace of regret. Outside, Vernon revealed that in all his years as a marketing executive with the tourist board, working with journalists and TV crews, this was the first time he'd actually had a chance to meet the great doctor. He thanked us. We thanked him. It seemed an auspicious start to our trip.

Our plan in Sri Lanka was not only to visit the places where Pa had served during the war but also to see some famous spots he was never able to get to. We especially wanted to take in the island's spectacular ruined Buddhist cities and temples. The road to the past, however, ran through the present. Cashew-nut sellers in bright saris beckoned to us as we drove north, and schoolchildren in neat white uniforms waved. We passed pineapple stalls, the Daily Needs grocery, the Walk Nice footwear store. There, plodding down the pavement on his way to haul hardwood, our first elephant. But far from our last. We broke the journey at the Pinnawala Elephant Orphanage, where the feeding and bathing rituals of fifty-five large, leathery residents filled us with unexpected joy. We were loath to depart and had to remind ourselves that most of these pachyderms were here because their mothers had been killed in an escalating conflict with villagers over dwindling areas of suitable habitat. One youngster attached her strong, flexible trunk to my camera strap, as if demanding I remain (or take her photo, at least).

On the dry northern plains, where many people still lived in thatched mud huts and went barefoot, we stopped at the ancient city of Anuradhapura and pondered a vast landscape of ruined statues, palaces, pagodas and "tanks," or artificial reservoirs, dating back more than two thousand years. The town's most famous site was a sacred fig tree, Sri Maha Bodhi, which had started life as a sapling cut from the original Bodhi tree in India, under which the Buddha was said to have achieved enlightenment. It had been looked after by an uninterrupted sequence of caretakers for more than two millennia. We collected fallen fig leaves, while pilgrims meditated or relaxed in the shade of the tree's foliage.

Vernon had brought books for a friend of his, the abbot of a local Buddhist monastery, who shook our hands and offered us tea. He spoke impeccable English and was surprisingly young, with a direct, serene gaze. Before we left, Vernon, an Anglican, knelt and asked for a blessing; the abbot chanted over him for a few moments, then tied a cotton thread round his right wrist. The incident struck me as emblematic of the country, where different faiths—Buddhism, Hinduism, Islam, Christianity—had coexisted (uneasily, perhaps, but continuously) for centuries. There was a syncretic quality to the spiritual life here: Hindus accepted the Buddha as a reincarnation of Vishnu; Muslims accepted Jesus as a great prophet of Allah. It made Sri Lanka's relentless, ongoing conflict between Tamils and Sinhalese all the more tragic and disturbing.

At Sigiriya, as recommended, we climbed the great fortress. We approached the monolith through peaceful water gardens, the air perfumed by frangipani blossoms, then passed between the paws of two gigantic stone lions. Adorning the walls as we ascended were fifth-century frescoes of half-clad maidens, as wasp-waisted and full-breasted as any Vargas pin-up. Sigiriya was really a testament to treachery; built by Kasyapa, who murdered his father to protect himself from his brother, the compact citadel and its penthouse palace had a kind of concentrated drama that made it one of Sri Lanka's most celebrated sites. From the summit, which you must reach by crossing a series of windswept grooves cut into the rock (there's a metal railing, but the climb is still a bit hair-raising), there was a grand panorama. You could sit on a stone throne, as Kasyapa must have done, searching the jungle for the mounted elephants of his brother's army, which eventually came and destroyed him.

On the way to Polonnaruwa, Sri Lanka's other great derelict metropolis, where huge Buddha images had been carved from a single ridge of granite, an excited motorcyclist put his arm in front of his face and made waving motions at us as he passed. Around the corner, a wild elephant was calmly stripping leaves from a roadside tree. At the cave temples of Dambulla, so cunningly painted that the rock walls seemed to undulate like rich, patterned fabric, we fended off monkeys and squinted through the gloom at golden statues. But at Mihintale, birthplace of Buddhism in Sri Lanka, we finally grew reluctant to haul our aching bones up any more flights of steps to any more relics. And at Kandy, high above sea level and refreshingly cool, we rested.

I'd mellowed, apparently, since 1980—or else I was more willing to look in the mirror—because Pa and I were travelling well together. We were close, but not demonstrative. We were competitive—hell, we both wrote books—but our rivalry was also a form of companionship, a sharing of common interests. Some part of me hoped this trip would result in a closer connection between us, a deeper understanding. We seemed suspended somehow in a subtle web of unspoken thoughts, unconscious agreements, unexplored feelings, unfinished business. We were old souls, with old obligations and old secrets, together again.

At Kandy, Sri Lanka's second-largest city, we were joined by Vernon's wife, Yvonne, and her sister-in-law Pushpa. Pa had been here before, when his commanding officer had given him a motorcycle and a few days off, and he'd headed for the hills. The Queen's Hotel, where he'd stayed—a venerable pile right in the centre of town overlooking Kandy's tranquil artificial lake—was still there, its genteel facade faded but correct. And the Peradeniya Botanic Gardens, where, in 1943, Lord Louis Mountbatten had been busy setting up the headquarters of the South East Asia Command, hadn't changed much in fifty years. Nice spot for a command post, I thought, up in the hills, surrounded by orchids and palms, well away from the heat.

Beyond Kandy, we followed the same route upcountry that Pa had taken on his motorbike—climbing past terraced rice paddies, then higher, through tea plantations that looked like green brain coral, then higher still, to vegetable country, where Tamil farmers tended leek and lettuce, radish and rhubarb. At nineteen hundred metres, Nuwara Eliya (pronounced nu-REL-iya), the favourite British hill station, was wet and foggy, as it had been when Pa was there in 1943. Unlike Captain Scott, who had pushed on in search of sunshine, we stuck around and checked into the Grand Hotel, a wood-panelled relic of Empire, complete with billiard room, fireplaces and a waiter named Muthu Banda, who had worked there for fifty-eight years and had served Queen Wilhelmina of the Netherlands in 1937.

Nuwara Eliya, with its pink post office, churches, horse track, country houses, gingerbread-trimmed cottages and lush, empty golf course, looked like a slice of Sussex plunked down in the jungle. We strolled over to the Hill Club, where the hallways were hung with hunting prints and gigantic stuffed trout (the British stocked hill-country waters with their favourite fish; the hatcheries still operated). A liveried attendant signed us up for a temporary membership, and we drank Lion Pilsners in the solitary splendour of the men's bar.

We had begun to develop a nice, relaxed rhythm on this journey, one of friends touring together. Just being able to meet and talk to so many Sri Lankans—a gentle, outgoing, physically beautiful people—had become our biggest pleasure. He hadn't been able to do this in wartime, my father regretted, because the army had kept itself aloof from the locals. But with Vernon's enthusiasm and knowledge, and with the van at our disposal, we were getting an intimate introduction to the culture—including the cuisine. The night before, for instance, I'd sampled snakeroot *sambol*, cuttlefish *badhum* and curries made from eggplant and immature jackfruit, all delicious.

For breakfast, we often stopped at government rest houses, where the menu included string hoppers, a kind of noodle served with curry, much loved by Sri Lankans. Many of these red-tiled bungalows, designed in a gracious Anglo-Indian architectural style with airy verandas and dining rooms and neoclassical trim, dated from the last century. The rest-house network was basically a system of simple, small-town hotels for travelling officials, and Pa was no stranger to them. Some were a bit rundown, but they were usually set in stunning locations: on a promontory with a view, perched beside a lake or ancient reservoir, or nestled snugly in the nicest curve of the best beach. The one at Ella, on the southern edge of the highlands, where you could dine alfresco surrounded by flowering shrubs and gaze through a gap in the hills right down to the coastal plain, topped the lot.

From the hill country we headed south to the beaches, spending the next few days visiting waterfalls and communing with wildlife. At Bundala National Park we took a jeep safari and saw marabou storks, ibises, spoonbills and dozens of other bird species, as well as monkeys and elephants. We also found elephants at Handapanagala, a sugar cane–producing area that had become something of a national *cause célèbre* when about 150 animals were cut off from the wildlife refuge at Yala by electrified fences set up to protect cane fields. They'd rampaged through the countryside, and both villagers and elephants had been killed.

Things were somewhat better at Yala itself, Sri Lanka's huge, southeastern national park. Again we saw elephants, including Kota, a big bull who had been coming for fifteen years to the back doors of the hotel kitchens for scraps. Only the previous year in Yala, however, two park rangers had been murdered by ivory poachers. Sri Lanka's slender economic means, seriously depleted by a long-running civil war (and, later, by a disastrous tidal wave), made it unable to devote sufficient resources to wildlife and environmental protection.

At Hambantota and Weligama on the south coast, an area that my father remembered well, we visited other rest houses, ones he had stayed at fifty years ago. As we cruised the island's famed beach resorts and I listened to old stories, I got the impression that life for a young army officer in wartime Ceylon, though constrained and often stressful, had not been unpleasant. The work—testing and calibrating the field guns, organizing jungle training for the troops—appeared to have left adequate time for swimming, and riding in outrigger fishing boats like the ones littering the beach at Hambantota. The island paradise of Ceylon had been a reprieve of sorts, because there would be no swimming in Burma, where the division was sent and saw action in 1943.

The final part of our quest was to find Matugama, an inland town, right off the tourist track. My father had been stationed there, at divisional headquarters—in the rest house, naturally. The question was: Would there be any traces from fifty years ago? I thought Pa was getting a little disappointed—not with Sri Lanka, which we both loved, but with memory itself, so unreliable, so deflating for one's expectations.

As we wandered around Matugama trying to identify old landmarks, the citizens, attentive but shy, treated us as minor curiosities, in the same league as the three-metre-long water monitor lizard that shuffled across the road just ahead. It looked fierce but it was harmless and so were we. We found the rest house boarded up. It had done such poor business, we were told, that the manager had been inspired to set up an illegal arak distillery on the premises. But he'd been caught, and now he languished in the local jail.

Nothing on this trip was turning out the way we'd expected. In truth, everything was better than we'd expected. But then, the island's old name was Serendip, from which came the word *serendipity*—the faculty of stumbling on good fortune by accident. What I'd stumbled on here was that this trip wasn't about needing to deepen the father-son bond, whatever that meant. It was simply about friendship. About reinvigorating ours. And about beginning a friendship (after appropriate parental introduction, of course) with the remote, romantic place that Marco Polo described as "undoubtedly the finest island of its size in all the world."

Thailand 1994

As the crowning touch for his Bangkok temple, the venerable Phra Viriyang Sirintharo sought an image of the Buddha that would last as long as the Enlightened One's teachings. For several years he and his followers had searched for the right material, considering and rejecting many different minerals and metals. The more he investigated, the more certain he became that only one substance—a scarce, beautiful, durable stone revered throughout Asia for millennia—would do justice to the Buddha and to the temple Wat Dhammamongkol. That substance was nephrite jade.

Settling on jade was one thing. Finding a piece large enough and fine enough to realize the image he had in mind was another thing entirely. The seventy-four-year-old lord abbot, affectionately known to everyone as Luang Phor ("respected father"), visited Myanmar and Canada and put the word out to other jade-producing regions. Then, in August 1991, he had a vision while meditating: a strange landscape of dwarfed trees and precipitous slopes under a vast empty sky. In a valley, an enormous weathered boulder lay by a stream, and he knew, with a deep certainty that was beyond thought, the boulder was jade.

Against the advice of his Thai supporters, Luang Phor prepared to fly across the Pacific and "just go look" for the boulder. A week later, quite independently, a fax arrived from a friend in Vancouver who knew of the temple's requirements. A British Columbia jade-mining company had unearthed the finest, largest piece of nephrite the company's president, a man named Kirk Makepeace, had ever seen. If Luang Phor was interested, he should come to Canada at once. The abbot smiled. The message did not surprise him.

My interest in jade was first fired by a report of this discovery in a business magazine. I learned, with surprise, that the world's largest and finest jade deposits were in northern BC, in my own vast backyard. The global market was only about three hundred tonnes a year, and two-thirds of this total was supplied by Jade West Resources, Makepeace's company, headquartered in Surrey, near Vancouver. Most BC jade went to China and Taiwan, where the best was used in jewellery and the rest carved into amulets, figurines, incense holders and the like. Some came back to BC in the form of beads, or tiny maple leaves, or bears with fish in their mouths, which were sold to tourists as souvenirs. Some never left the country and was fashioned instead into expensive sculptures by a select group of artists. As I read about the mineral's glamorous history and mythology, I felt myself being drawn, as many had before me, into jade's mysterious orbit. I determined to follow, if I could,

Opposite: A river crossing in northern Thailand.

the gemstone's trail from Canadian source to Asian finished product.

For Luang Phor, the quest for jade was the beginning of an adventurous relationship with Canada. He visited Vancouver for Expo 86 and made several other trips, travelling to the BC jade mines and getting to know the Canadian Thai community. In 1992, he founded Yanviriya Temple—Canada's first Thai-style Buddhist wat—in East Vancouver, and soon after, he opened another wat in Toronto. Later, temples would also be established in Ottawa, Niagara Falls, Calgary and Edmonton. Although the wats were designed for local Thai Buddhists, anyone could attend meditation classes and prayer services, and visitors were always welcome.

After receiving the fax about the new find, Luang Phor made an immediate trip to Jade West's South Surrey yard. Several buyers, including a Beijing jade dealer, were interested in the thirty-two-tonne boulder, which had been cut into three compact car–sized chunks so that it could be transported from the mines. This was Polar Jade, which took a superior polish, according to Makepeace, and was harder and clearer than normal nephrite. The abbot decided then and there that the pieces were what he'd been looking for, paid for them and had them shipped to Thailand. The $360,000 transaction was the largest sale ever of BC jade and strengthened Canada's reputation as the leading producer and exporter of the semi-precious stone. It also cemented Kirk Makepeace's status as the country's most astute jade hunter.

Now came the difficult part: finding someone who could turn the ungainly, viridescent blocks into powerful images. Few Thai artists carved jade anymore. Rather than commission Chinese artisans, who had fashioned smaller jade Buddhas for Chinese temples, Luang Phor travelled to Carrara, Italy, a city famous for its marble sculptors. There he hired Zizi Smail and Paolo Viaggi. Neither artist had worked in jade before, and both initially found that their marble-carving tools and techniques were not up to the task. After experimenting for two months to find the right equipment, then spending nine steamy, strenuous months cutting, grinding and sanding, they completed the work. Another month was spent in polishing.

"After this," Viaggi said to Luang Phor, "marble will seem like butter."

Jade had been sculpted and treasured for more than thirty-five hundred years in Southeast Asia. Most of the region's oldest-known carvings were of nephrite jade, a silicate of calcium, magnesium and iron. BC jade was nephrite. A brighter, rarer type of jade—a silicate of sodium and aluminum—also existed: jadeite, sacred to the ancient cultures of Central America. Both jades came in white, red, blue, black and yellow, as well as the trademark range of greens, which had picked up such poetic names as kingfisher, moss, melon peel and spinach.

What gave nephrite special value, beyond the subtle beauty of its coloration, was its toughness. Composed of fibrous crystals tightly matted and locked together, nephrite took fine detail when carved. It polished to a rich glow, was hard enough to resist accidental abrasion and was just about impossible to shatter. Nephrite sculptures, while notoriously difficult to work and time-consuming to polish, lasted a long, long time.

Nephrite was highly regarded wherever it was found. In New Zealand, for instance, the Maori people knew the mineral as *pounamu*, or greenstone, and fashioned it into neck and earlobe pendants and amulets, chisels and adzes, and clubs.

Nephrite became an important trade item in North America, where it was carved into a variety of tools and household objects. George Mercer Dawson, legendary director of the Geological Survey of Canada, who gave his name to Dawson City, made extensive travels in northwestern British Columbia in 1887 and noted nephrite's widespread occurrence. According to the anthropologist George Emmons, the mineral was not fashioned into personal ornaments in BC, which was strange, considering its ceremonial use elsewhere in the ancient world.

"Jade had no religious significance, nor was it regarded with superstition," wrote Emmons in a 1923 monograph on the prehistory of North American jade. "But a certain sentiment seemed to attach to it wherever found."[5]

The Taoist and Buddhist cultures of China and Southeast Asia—those parts of the world we instinctively associate with jade—brought homage of the mineral to its peak. Nephrite was honoured there as the "stone of heaven"—

a symbolic link between life and immortality. It represented charity, justice and wisdom.

Despite a long history of use, nephrite was not plentiful in China. Steady demand first sent Chinese jade buyers to Burma, then farther afield, to new mines in Siberia, Taiwan and Korea. Nephrite existed in Australia, Europe, Africa and Brazil—all around the world, in fact. Excellent stone was found in California, Wyoming and Alaska. But for production to succeed, three conditions had to be satisfied—high quality, sufficient quantity and reasonable ease of access. This happened only rarely. And the place that best satisfied these conditions was northern BC.

As we waited for our charter flight to Jade West's Kutcho Creek mine, 420 kilometres to the north, we admired a gorgeous, twin-engined 1948 Beech Eighteen that looked as if it had flown straight from the set of a Humphrey Bogart film. We were at Smithers, one of several jumping-off spots and supply depots for BC's northern wilderness. It was ten o'clock in the morning, and Vancouver was already 700 kilometres behind us. Besides Kirk Makepeace and me, Luang Phor was also making the journey, together with Peter Utokaparch, a lay follower from Vancouver who would serve as interpreter. Chris Oben and Don Killen, a two-man video crew, were there to document the story behind yet another jade boulder that Luang Phor had just purchased. I had a magazine assignment to write an article about BC's expanding jade trade.

When it was announced that we'd be travelling to Kutcho in the ancient Beech, a certain nervousness prevailed, but any misgivings we may have felt about the age of the aircraft were soon dispelled by the fine July weather and the scenery. The pilot, Gary Meier, sped us smoothly past the headwaters of the Skeena, across the verdant Spatsizi Plateau and over the swirling Stikine River. We saw caribou cooling off on mountaintop snow patches but precious few signs of man. These north-central BC highlands, home to rich deposits of jade, were the heart of the wild.

Eventually, a gravel airstrip materialized in a wide, lush valley. Of all the peaks we could see, only the highest—2,400-metre King Mountain—rated a name on our topographic map, which described the airfield as "condition unknown." In reality, it was the best in the region, lengthened, upgraded and connected by a rough dirt road to the small community of Dease Lake, ninety kilometres west.

The Jade West camp was right beside the runway, surrounded by old chunks of rough-cut jade. Elizabeth Greenough, the camp cook, was on hand to greet us, and the rest of the crew, including the mine manager, Tony Ritter, soon drove up from the mine site, seven kilometres away. In no time at all, we were consuming an enormous dinner of roast turkey and apple pie. The mine employees worked ten hours a day, seven days a week, hurrying against winter to extract enough jade to keep the company going for the rest of the year. In September, giant-wheeled, all-terrain vehicles would haul the season's best boulders to Dease Lake, from which point they would be trucked south over the paved Stewart-Cassiar Highway.

The next morning, we crowded into a well-used Toyota Land Cruiser and bounced over a toad of a road to visit the mine. The valley bottom was matted with low willow and birch shrubs. There were wildflowers in profusion: monkshood, paintbrush, red columbine, bluebells and harebells, fireweed and river beauty, purple aster and feathery tufts of mountain avens. Brave armies of gnarled, stunted white spruce and subalpine fir marched up the mountainsides but soon surrendered, leaving the terrain to marmots and rock ptarmigan. Kutcho Creek rippled through the valley, its clear, icy waters teeming with trout.

A definite spirit of excitement—jade fever, if you will—began to grip our small group. Oben, Killen and I were becoming connoisseurs of discarded jade fragments. Makepeace, forty-one, skipped around his domain like a mountain goat and seemed to get younger and younger as the day progressed. As we drew near the jade operation, even Luang Phor showed signs of losing his Buddhist cool. "Do you ever in place like this before?" he whispered to me in broken English, rubbing his hands in anticipation. "This true adventure!"

Below a rocky ridge, at the foot of a steep slope of glaucous scree, the crew was working a vein or "lens" of jade. "This is serpentine," said Makepeace, fingering a piece of loose, grey-green talus, "and BC has lots of it."

He explained that jade often formed where a layer of serpentine was squeezed against a harder bedrock, such as granite, by the movement of the earth's crust. Over thousands of years, heat and pressure might cause a layer of serpentine to metamorphose into something tougher and more compact—like jade. As the softer surrounding serpentine gradually eroded, the thin band of jade, usually less than two metres wide, would be exposed.

Makepeace pointed to a dark olive stripe that snaked through the ridge high above us. "We call that the China Wall." Discovered in 1969 by a local prospector named Andy Jensen, it was perhaps the richest deposit of jade on the planet.

"There's thousands of tonnes of jade up there," Makepeace continued, "enough to supply the world for centuries. But it would be incredibly expensive to mine. What we've done is trace that vein down to where we can get at it. ... This kind of mining is ideal for a small operator with an intimate knowledge of the business. Quality is everything, and the work has to be babied along, which is probably why big corporate concerns haven't succeeded."

At the base of the ridge, an excavator and bulldozer had cleared away tonnes of serpentine to reveal, in Tony Ritter's words, "a wall of jade standing upright." The twenty-eight-year-old manager was feeling confident.

"The jade is proven," he said. "We just have to extract it. Sometimes the jade is no good, so we've done a lot of work for nothing. Or the quality can change as we work along a seam. Or the site may become too difficult or expensive or dangerous to work. We're never quite sure what we're going to get. You have to develop an instinct for jade."

On a flat bit of ground near the face of the seam, dozens of jade boulders, roughly broken off with the excavator bucket, had been laid out. A pair of huge diesel saws with diamond-edged blades were slowly cutting them into manageable sizes, removing the dross and revealing smooth faces of shining stone so that potential buyers could judge colour and quality for themselves.

Makepeace eagerly inspected the new trophies. "High-quality jade is translucent and bright, and apple or emerald green in colour," he explained. "It has no inclusions, fractures or soft spots. This is some of the best we've ever had."

Jade West separated its product into four grades—AA, A, B and C—and priced it according to quality, amount purchased and whether the individual blocks were rough-cut or trimmed. The price of BC jade varied greatly, anywhere from $200 to $2,000 per kilogram.

Polar Jade, sold mostly to jewellers and sculptors, was mined at a site thirty-two kilometres west of Kutcho Creek. The company also mined jade at Ogden Mountain, northeast of Smithers, owned a small rhodonite operation on the north BC coast and would be managing a lapis lazuli mine in Chile that winter. (Rhodonite, mauve in colour, and lapis, which is a rich, dark blue, are also semi-precious minerals, mined in similar fashion to jade.)

By buying out several key competitors, Jade West had emerged as the market's leading player. But big was still small, especially compared with the huge operations most Canadians associate with the word *mining*. *Mining* wasn't even a good word to describe what Jade West did; *quarrying* was more like it. Nevertheless, the work had a significant environmental impact. The company would have to regrade all its mine sites and access roads, then seed disturbed areas with a special grass that stabilized the ground and allowed native vegetation to regrow. Environmental bonds had been posted so that if Jade West went out of business, money would still be there for restoration work.

The art of creating large Buddha figures from jade, once confined to Southeast Asia, was becoming a global phenomenon. A Polar Jade boulder found by Kirk Makepeace in northern BC in 2000, for instance, valued at $1.5 million, ended up at the Great Stupa of Universal Compassion in Bendigo, Australia. Modelled on a statue in the Mahabodhi Temple, in Bodh Gaya, India (where the Buddha is said to have achieved enlightenment), it was carved by the Jade Thongtavee Company in Chiang Rai, one of Thailand's last traditional jade factories. The original stone weighed eighteen tonnes; the 2.5-metre-high finished image, which was consecrated by the Dalai Lama and made a world tour between 2009 and 2014, tipped the scales at four tonnes.

Another jade boulder from northern BC was purchased by the Vancouver entrepreneur and philanthropist Jim Houston, who hired Lyle Sopel, a local jade artist, to sculpt a meditating Buddha inspired by Luang Phor's Wat Dhammamongkol statue. By the time Sopel had finished this naturalistic figure, in 2003, he had whittled the

900-kilogram boulder down to 350 kilos. Houston died in 2018, and Uno Langmann Fine Art had the Buddha for sale recently for $950,000. Alternatively, if you found the price a little on the high side, you could purchase a 220-kilogram fat laughing Buddha from Vancouver's Jade Store for a mere $28,000.

China likely had more giant jade Buddhas on display than any other country. Several of the oldest and most famous were in Shanghai: the seated Buddha at Jing'an Temple, for instance, and the sitting and reclining Buddhas, originally from Burma, at the Jade Buddha Temple. These were all sculpted from white jade, which was valued almost as highly in China as green. A 65-tonne white jade statue at the Meishansi nunnery in Amoy (Xiamen) was also a contender for largest Buddha. A 260-tonne figure in the northeast Chinese city of Anshan, however—a protected heritage property and "treasure of the state," often said to be the world's largest jade Buddha—was carved from serpentine, not jade.

During a 1994 trip to Thailand, I visited Wat Phra Kaew, adjoining Bangkok's Grand Palace, to see the Emerald Buddha, the most famous ornamental Buddha of them all. Confusingly, the sixty-six-centimetre-tall statue was not made of emerald or jade, but of a green-coloured, semi-precious mineral called jasper. According to legend, whoever possessed the Emerald Buddha inherited a god-given right to rule. Over the centuries the sculpture had become a supreme spoil of war, moving with its latest owner around Laos and northern Thailand, until it finally came to rest in Bangkok.

Less reliable legends held that the carving had been created more than two thousand years ago in India. It spent time in Ceylon, where it helped avert a civil war, then was shipwrecked off the coast of Cambodia and lost for many years before resurfacing in Thailand. Centuries later, the pampered figure acquired three sets of decorative clothing—for summer, winter and the rainy season—all made from pure gold studded with sapphires and other precious gems. The outfits were changed by the king of Thailand or a senior member of the royal family every March, August and November. In the old days the Emerald Buddha had been taken out of the wat in times of disaster and marched through the streets in the belief that its presence would help alleviate any catastrophe.

After my visit, I went to Wat Dhammamongkol to see the world's latest and largest jade Buddha and interview Luang Phor. The wat was enormous; its twelve-storey tower, with a museum on top and served by an elevator, loomed over Bangkok's eastern suburbs. It was also home to a career development centre (cooking, dressmaking, carving, computers) and a radio station. Wary of the city's infamous traffic, I arrived early and spent an hour being quizzed by curious novice monks about subtleties in the English language. How could they be sure they were using the imperfect and pluperfect tenses correctly? Could a Canadian writer explain such things to them?

At last the abbot arrived and saved the writer from further embarrassment, and I was taken to a bright pavilion shaped like a geodesic dome, roofed in clear glass and finished in marble. At the heart of this ceremonial space, the harsh Asian sunlight played over a gleaming statue more than two metres tall. The ten-tonne figure, carved with such difficulty from dark green stone, had been fashioned in a formal meditation pose, cross-legged, hands folded in lap. At the back of the pavilion, an alcove was being readied for a second jade statue, this one of Guan Yin, the Buddhist goddess of mercy. Beneath the pavilion, workers were busy finishing construction of a huge, two-storey columbarium, with space for sixty thousand crematory urns.

Luang Phor, as energetic as a man half his age, was, as usual, having a busy day. He had started planning this wat in the early 1960s, after growing up in a rural village in north-east Thailand, where he suffered as a child from a mysterious paralysis. He recovered, vowed in gratitude to become a Buddhist monk and spent twenty years at a forest retreat before moving to Bangkok and settling in a thatched hut in a swampy area where his "only neighbours were snakes." Now Wat Dhammamongkol rose where his hut once stood, and Luang Phor had gone on to build daycare centres, temples and hospitals around the world. Finding and installing the jade Buddha celebrated a lifetime of work.

"I chose the most permanent material in the world as a symbol for the long-lasting teachings of the Buddha," Luang Phor told me through an interpreter. "I decided to create the biggest possible image in order to attract attention. People will come and pay respect and be attracted to the teachings of the Buddha. I have devoted my life to the Buddha and learned how good his teachings are for mankind. I would like other people to be able to experience the same thing."

By late September, things were getting frantic at Jade West's Surrey yard. This year's jade had been trucked down from the mines, local artists had chosen what they wanted from the freshly cut stone, and now buyers were arriving from Taiwan and China to look over the rest of the boulders. While BC carvers took only about ten tonnes of jade a year, Makepeace tried to give them first pick. It was his way of boosting Canada's chances of being known as something more than a mere supplier of raw jade.

Because Jade West controlled the market, Makepeace could price the high-grade jade so people "couldn't make bears with fish in their mouths out of it." With the market stable, jade entrepreneurs could focus on developing new uses for their product. Makepeace saw a future for jade industrial goods, like tiles, tabletops and fireplace facings. "Jade makes a perfect tile," he said. "It's strong, durable and beautiful." Demand for jade was expanding steadily. Europe was becoming a presence in the market. Thailand, with a dozen jade Buddhas in the making, was a major buyer. Even New Zealand was importing BC jade. The year's business looked excellent, according to Makepeace, with prices holding firm. Despite having a large stock of jade on hand, he now wished he'd mined an extra hundred tonnes.

Luang Phor's latest boulder, which had been accidentally uncovered in an ancient stream bed, was also sitting in the Surrey yard. Rounded and smoothed by centuries of stream immersion, its surface was free of the dull, greyish oxidization that normally built up. Its rich, green hue was plain for all to see.

This boulder was not destined to become a Buddha. In fact, it would not even be leaving the country. It would remain in its natural shape and would be brought to a pinnacle of polish by a high-pressure water jet, then taken to Luang Phor's latest Canadian temple and meditation centre, a 105-year-old former Catholic church recently acquired in Niagara Falls. There the stone of heaven would be on permanent display. "It came from Canada," said Luang Phor, "and I am going to leave it in Canada, because I wish to give something back."

Phra Viriyang Sirintharo (Luang Phor) celebrated his one hundredth birthday in January 2020.

India 1993 and 1995

The first few days in India were overwhelming. I knew this to be a common experience for newcomers; no amount of travelling prepared you for the poverty, the crowds and the dust. For the past month I'd been travelling with friends in Sri Lanka, but now I was alarmingly alone. The weather was unbearable: hot, close, wet. Accommodation, transport, food—everything was a hassle. Maybe I'll just give up, I thought, and retreat somewhere safer.

I was having this minor breakdown in a place called Kollam (or Quilon, as it was once known). One thousand years ago, it had been one of the main spice-trading ports on the fabled Malabar Coast, but now it was rundown and nondescript—just another overpopulated city in the state of Kerala, a narrow strip of fertile land clinging to the south-western coast of India.

I was here because Kollam was the southern terminus for a series of ferry trips one could make along the coast via an elaborate labyrinth of backwater canals and lagoons. My imagination (and reports from other travellers) had convinced me that this would be a relaxed way to explore the gentle landscapes of Kerala and investigate its unusual history.

In the Hindu religion, Nandi the bull is sacred to Lord Shiva. This massive tribute to Nandi is in the city of Mysore, India.

Only I'd arrived on the wrong damned day.

The schedule had changed. The government ferry didn't leave until the day after tomorrow. I was stuck in nowheresville, where the best hotel cost four dollars a night. On the ferry dock I sank into a spiral of woe, before finally beginning to talk myself out of it. Things could be worse (just look around you). You have money. You are healthy. Accept the situation.

As I prepared to leave, a man approached and told me that if he could find a minimum of six passengers, a private boat would leave tomorrow morning for Alappuzha (Alleppey), the next city along the coast. It was more expensive, he said, looking at me hesitantly: six dollars instead of a buck and a half for the eight-hour trip. This was a new thing, not in the guidebook yet. Be there at eight and don't be late. My spirits perked up cautiously and I wandered back into town.

Something had changed. Before, I'd seen beggars and filth. Now I saw smiling faces selling pineapples and purple grapes. For the future, I must remember: in India there was always another boat. Now I was smiling also, and two young brothers, banana wholesalers, welcomed me into their shop. They were unloading and arranging giant stalks of fruit: sweet bananas, red bananas, big cooking plantains. They posed humorously, hamming it up for a photo.

The vegetable vendors had orange squash, bright green marrows, leeks, eggplants and burlap sacks of dried red chilies. There were wicker baskets of apples and limes and gooseberries. A merchant was packing an enormous bag of rice into a trishaw's tiny passenger seat, already occupied by a woman and child. I bought supplies for the trip: banana chips, delicious little deep-fried rice cakes, fruit, chocolate.

Along the main street a large store specialized just in paper, all different sizes and types and colours—mostly for wrapping things, I guessed. Another merchant sold only stainless-steel kitchen and household utensils; water jugs and basins were arranged around his doorway in a gleaming, mirrored arch. A man sat on the sidewalk preparing red betel paste—a popular mild stimulant—and folding each tooth-staining dose in a green, heart-shaped leaf. Another man rolled and sold bidis—Indian cigarettes, wrapped in a single ebony leaf and tied with a red thread.

As daylight faded, I came to a crossroads and stopped. Throngs of people poured past me on the dusky street. I was mesmerized. Women in bright saris fluttered around the stalls. Families promenaded. Young men lounged in lungis, old men in dhotis, talking, smoking. Sitar music drifted out of a nearby store. The eerie half-light picked out the gleam of a metal utensil, a flash of jewellery. Flames flickered at portable cooking carts, where little pancakes called dosas were being fried and cashew nuts roasted.

For twenty minutes I stood there, entranced, part of the dense human mass. I didn't fit in, of course, but no one paid me any heed. It was the purest magic. Somehow the hours of inconvenience and sweat had become worthwhile. What, I wondered, would tomorrow bring?

Tomorrow, it turned out, brought sunshine and a dozen travellers, each happy to pay six dollars for a slow boat through Kerala. We were a friendly group—French, German, British, Canadian and Indian—and we reclined on the roof of the ten-metre *Calicut* (operated by the Alleppey Tourism Development Co-operative Society) with our snacks and cameras for a multilingual chat.

For two hundred kilometres, a maze of shallow inland waterways stretched north along the coast. Two centuries of human labour had turned this natural formation into a well-used, interconnected transportation network. As the day progressed, we passed hundreds of workmen fine-tuning the channels from their dugouts, dredging mud by hand, transporting it from place to place, strengthening the banks, building up the shoreline to create new land.

We met an amazing variety of craft: fishing boats, other ferries and flat-bottomed cargo vessels, some flaunting well-patched sails, some with rattan roofs to protect rice and produce. Tiny dugouts provided service across the channels; passengers usually stood, the women holding black umbrellas. Fast-moving, fifteen-metre dragon boats passed, their high black prows draped with strips of cloth for luck. Powered by several outboard motors rigged to the side, the ones I saw held mounds of netting and at least twenty fishermen.

Hundreds of large cantilevered fishing nets (known as Chinese nets, after their inventors) lined the shallows, suspended like immense stick insects above wooden platforms.

They were used at night at high tide, when the net was submerged beneath a bright light, which attracted fish, then scooped up quickly. Hawks, eagles and terns wheeled overhead, while ibises and long-legged marsh herons probed the lily and lotus patches.

Travelling over the endless, shimmering waters in this languid fashion was like moving through a dream. It was perfect for observing the day-to-day activities of the inhabitants, which had the quality of a slow, steady dance. Rural women, their arms resting on parallel, chest-high poles, threshed rice with their feet. Others sat in groups beneath the palm trees, separating coir (coconut fibre) from husks that were first softened in water. Across the canal, a man turned a simple wheel, spinning the coir into coarse rope.

The cadent patterns of the human body at work were repeated everywhere: corn was ground by mortar and pestle; hand nets were thrown out and hauled back in; poles were endlessly planted and pushed by muscular men who walked the flat gunwales of the vessels, propelling them across the lagoons. At the water's edge, women pounded their washing to an ancient rhythm. Even pedestrians on the canal paths strode in perfect harmony.

The land was flat and green and fertile, prime coconut and rice-growing territory, with a healthy scattering of mango and cashew trees. Famous in antiquity as the Malabar Coast, the region had welcomed the world's traders for three thousand years. Phoenicians, Romans, Arabs and Chinese had visited here in search of spices, sandalwood and ivory. When Europeans arrived—first the Portuguese, then the Dutch and the British—they found a sophisticated culture receptive to newcomers and open to foreign ideas. Later, red hammers and sickles decorated many walls.

Because this agricultural panorama still largely lacked any motorized equipment, life appeared to have a timeless quality. The view we got from the roof of the *Calicut* hadn't changed much in centuries. But it was a misleading view in some ways, because Kerala was one of India's most progressive states and had changed greatly in the past fifty years. Everywhere in South Asia you heard about the "Kerala miracle."

The region's former maharajas, instead of exploiting their subjects and living high off the proceeds, had laid a responsible groundwork for public education and health care. Infant mortality was the lowest in India. The literacy rate, at more than ninety percent, was the highest, nearly double the country's average. Life expectancy was eleven years longer than the norm, and the birth rate was less than two percent, close to that of Canada. Keralan women had long taken advantage of free public schooling on an equal basis with men (very unusual in India). Land reform had been peaceably accomplished by a freely elected Communist legislature that had governed Kerala for many years.

All this despite the state's thirty-million population in an area smaller than Switzerland and its per capita income of less than $500 a year. Here, poverty was not necessarily synonymous with suffering. As we moved through the countryside or bought tea and samosas at brief pit stops, the people greeted us with warmth and dignity. Outside the schools, children ran to the banks to wave. But to most observers, we were neither a novelty nor a symbol of oppression; we were neither envied nor scorned. We were just the latest boatload of backwater travellers, floating through eternity.

We arrived at Alappuzha at dusk, India's magic hour, when work was finished and people were taking it easy. Entering the city's canal system, we passed crowded state ferries on their way to other towns. My day on the water had relaxed me. Somehow I'd managed to slip into the flow, leaving my judgments and fear temporarily behind in some side channel. I found a good Indian-style hotel: cold water and squat toilet only, but impeccably clean and with a fine restaurant. An experimental plunge into the menu was rewarded with delectable chicken masala, vegetable korma, tasty parathas and a cool Kingfisher beer.

Alappuzha was located at the heart of the backwater region. Its old nickname, Venice of the East, may no longer be appropriate, but it still had a lively crossroads feel. A famous regatta took place there every August, with long, low-slung snake boats competing for the Nehru Cup. After dinner, I ventured into the busy streets and came across a folklore performance in a school courtyard. Regional dance styles—such as Kathakali, which had evolved from the most archaic temple rites—were followed by cool teenagers in shades and gloves doing Michael Jackson imitations. A fight broke out in the audience. Friendly competition, my neighbour explained, moving away smartly.

Early the next morning, I was down at the public dock, deciphering the schedules of the State Water Transport Department ferries. These were big, dirty, exhausted-looking wooden vessels that each carried about two hundred passengers. I caught one to Kottayam, a three-hour trip through more canals and across Vembanad Lake. The ferry was the local bus, complete with ticket collector. It stopped on request at tiny landings, the boatmen manoeuvring their substantial craft with bamboo poles, and slowed down politely to avoid swamping heavily loaded dugouts, which often had only a centimetre or two of freeboard.

We saw cross-topped churches along the way, pink or white against the deep blue sky. When the great Portuguese explorer Vasco da Gama had arrived on the Keralan coast in 1498, he found Christianity well established. Saint Thomas the Apostle was said to have landed there in AD 52 (the earliest Christian church ruins had been dated to the fourth century). There were many Syrian Christians around the rubber-producing town of Kottayam; their ancestors had first arrived in AD 190. By the time of my visit, twenty percent of Kerala's population was Christian, with another twenty percent Muslim and the rest Hindu.

The ramshackle Kottayam ferry dock was at the end of a cul-de-sac choked by water hyacinths. A line of trishaws awaited disembarking passengers. I headed straight to the train station, where I just caught the midday express to Kochi (Cochin), one of India's most fascinating cities. Until recently, you could have travelled from Alappuzha to Kochi by boat, a twenty-four-hour journey, but this service had apparently been discontinued. Kochi, however, was definite backwater country.

The city, with a population of about one million, was spread across a cluster of islands and peninsulas. Kochi was a famous port and major naval base, and visitors could not help but get a good look at its magnificent harbour: the different neighbourhoods could be reached only by an elaborate local ferry system. Kochi was a wonderful place to end one's Keralan travels; all the state's eclectic influences and historical associations were gathered there in one location.

The more modern part of the city, across the harbour on the mainland and known as Ernakulam, bustled with bright lights, hotels and restaurants. But the winding, five-hundred-year-old streetscapes of Fort Kochi and Mattancherry out among the islands still conveyed a medieval atmosphere. You could visit India's oldest operational church, Saint Francis, built in 1503 by Portuguese Franciscans. It contained the tomb of Vasco da Gama, who died in Kochi and was buried there, but whose remains were later transferred to Lisbon. The Portuguese also built Mattancherry Palace, where the walls were covered with extraordinary murals depicting scenes from Hindu epic literature.

The most intriguing, unexpected part of Kochi was near Mattancherry. Here, at the heart of a latticework of ancient alleys, were vestiges of a Jewish community that dated back to the first century and had been involved in the spice trade. There was a synagogue, constructed in

1568. The community was virtually extinct today, but the district's Indian merchants continued to trade in spice and coir and grain, and as I wandered past the decrepit buildings, many still emblazoned with the Star of David, the air was pungent with ginger, cardamom, cumin and clove.

Preoccupied with my camera, I was startled to find a young man at my elbow, with an invitation to meet his family and have tea. He led me into one of the old buildings, where, sure enough, his parents, wife, son and three nieces and nephews joined us. They were the Ahmeds, spice merchants who did most of their business with the Middle East and were affluent enough to employ three servants. Balquis, the young man's father, showed me the spacious, comfortable house: ground-floor "godown" for storage, family quarters on the second floor, third floor reserved for guests and an office. Out back was the spice-drying yard.

As we talked about life in India and Canada, the afternoon grew long. I began to grow nervous about catching the ferry back to my Ernakulam hotel. Balquis urged me to stay and have something to eat. I hesitated. The social setting was unfamiliar and I was a long way from home. Don't worry, said Balquis; in India, there is always another boat.

1995

The flight from Singapore arrived at Madras (now known as Chennai) at an ungodly hour in the morning. I wasn't expecting Katherine to meet me at the airport, but as I stumbled out of the terminal I was thrilled to find her expectant and slightly anxious face waiting in the crowd. She was looking elegant in a purple kameez and churidars: a long tunic over pyjama-style trousers. I was looking ... well, like I'd just taken an overnight flight in a lunch box.

We were relieved beyond words to see each other. Katherine, especially, had taken quite a risk in agreeing to meet me in such an unlikely spot. Although we had spent a lot of time together over the last few months, our relationship was still fairly new. Our plan to travel around southern India for six weeks was, according to a few of our friends, somewhat insane. We knew it would be a test, but a test was what we were looking for; if we could survive—and enjoy—this journey, we thought, then we should be able to make a success of cohabitation. We wanted to bring our friendship to a new level, and India was to be the proving ground.

We had plenty in common, certainly, including a deep interest in travel. Katherine was a busy freelance journalist, a talented artist and photographer, a spokesperson for a writers' association and a part-time worker at the Travel Bug, a popular travel bookstore in Vancouver, where I frequently found myself dropping by for a chat. And we were fascinated by India; this was her third trip and my second. A few days ago she'd been in Assam, at Kaziranga National Park, searching for rhinoceroses from the back of an elephant.

After a day of recovery in Madras we hopped onto a bus headed for Mahabalipuram, a UNESCO World Heritage location on the shores of the Indian Ocean, not far south. We rented bicycles for two days and explored the sights, the most famous of which was a huge, open-air, seventh-century relief, carved into two monolithic boulders, that celebrated the legendary history of the divine river Ganges. To the annoyance of the ruin's custodians, a tribe of sure-footed goats had taken up residence on the carving's sheer walls. They appeared to be enjoying a group of performers playing avant-garde music on a nearby stage. We visited the eighth-century Tiger Cave, the entrance guarded by stone tiger heads; two delicate shore temples, decorated with images of Nandi, the sacred bull; and the *ratha* temples, carved right out of the bedrock in the shapes of chariots. In town we shopped for small stone carvings, which were a specialty of the area. You could watch the sculptors work—and listen to them too, as their rhythmic hammers tink-tink-tinked away in the background. I found a small meditating Buddha that appealed to me. The owner of the stall explained that his teenaged son had made this piece, that it wasn't perfect. Would I like to see other work, as well? I was diplomatic and bought a miniature Buddha head from the father, which watches over me as I write these words, but the son's figure has always been my favourite.

A high point of travel in India, for both of us, was the food. Breakfast in Mahabalipuram, for instance, included fresh fruits and masala dosa (rice and lentil crepes with spiced potato stuffing) or idli (steamed lentil rice cakes), served outside in a shady bower. Beside us was a big pond where frogs splashed and skittered over hyacinth leaves and hungry kingfishers gathered. The southern cuisine was largely vegetarian, which was fine with us. The emphasis on rice suited Katherine, who was gluten intolerant. At dinner we sampled a variety of piquant stews (sambar), curries, rice biryanis and tamarind-flavoured soups, with side dishes of raita, a yogurt-based sauce. Flying Eagle beer became a cherished beverage.

There were wonderful seafoods, of course: ginger prawns, fried pomfret and snapper, tuna grilled with lemon and garlic. But these were special treats. We became very conscious of the contrast between our tourist lifestyle and that of the people who lived here, most of whom could not dream of dining on such expensive delicacies as prawns and tuna. I'd had this lesson drilled into my head on my first visit to India, when, stumbling home after enjoying a late-night seafood feast with spur-of-the-moment travel companions, I walked past a man bedded down on the sidewalk on his dirty piece of cardboard. He lifted his head. "Ah, sahib," he said, in stately English, "have you eaten well this evening?" Startled, I muttered something affirmative. "That is good to hear," he replied, then rolled over and turned his back to me.

Our next stop was the old French colony of Puducherry, a hundred kilometres farther south on the Coromandel Coast, where the famous alternative community of Auroville was located. I'd arranged to interview one of the residents, a man named Bill Sullivan, at the Auroville Centre for Scientific Research. He was going to tell me about the wonders of biogas.

The scorching midday sun had forced us into the shade of a large ferro-cement cylinder, part of an organic refuse digester manufactured on the premises and designed to be sunk into the ground. This one, said Sullivan, was a family-sized model: put in two buckets of kitchen slops, garden waste and human or animal excrement, and out came two buckets of processed fertilizer plus enough methane to fuel a stove for five hours.

Biogas was marvellous technology. It was simple, cheap and efficient: a combined garbage-disposal and power-generation plant that didn't pollute or even smell bad. For a developing country like India, in desperate need of practical, low-tech, renewable sources of energy, it was ideal. Biogas was a good example of a favourite Sullivan buzzword: "appropriate" technology. And appropriate technology was what Sullivan's adopted home was all about.

The international experiment of Auroville—a utopia of sorts—had been born in 1968, when handfuls of earth from around the world were symbolically mingled in an inaugural urn. "Auroville wanted to be a universal township," said its introductory brochure, "where men and women of all countries are able to live in peace and progressive harmony, above all creeds, all politics and all nationalities. The purpose of Auroville is to realize human unity."

Although its growth had been slow, the universal township, located about ten kilometres from central Puducherry, seemed alive and well. Its eight hundred members—about four hundred Indian, one hundred French and the rest drawn from twenty-five other nations—lived in more than thirty different settlements spread over one thousand hectares of semi-tropical forest. They coexisted and co-operated with several adjacent villages, which were not part of the community. While Auroville was far from being a tourist attraction, visitors were welcome and could stay at many of the settlements. Indeed, some never left.

Back at the Centre for Scientific Research, Sullivan, who was originally from the US but had lived in India for twenty-one years, showed us a few of the other appropriate technologies he and his colleagues were working on: solar water heaters and cookers, windmills, ferro-cement housing components and hand-operated presses for making unfired "earth blocks," a favourite Auroville building material that consisted mostly of earth with a little cement added. Then he sent us across the road to Auromodal, where garments were produced in a series of attractive airy buildings. From there, we got directions to a settlement specializing in reforestation and agriculture.

As we zipped over the red dirt roads on our rented scooter, the fruits of reforestation were all around us. Thirty years ago, this region was an overgrazed wasteland. Today, after a massive volunteer effort that saw more than a million saplings planted, we travelled under a lush canopy of coconut palms and guava, mango, jackfruit and cashew trees. We passed by minicommunities with names like Aspiration, which was devoted to education, health care and village economy; Fraternity (handicrafts); Meadow (tree planting); and Discipline (agriculture). Some were strikingly housed in innovative buildings, others hidden away down winding paths. We soon realized that we were quite lost—and hungry to boot.

Fortunately, we made this discovery close to a group of structures that turned out to include a bakery, an organic produce store and an area where local women were working at sewing machines and where lunch had been prepared. For forty cents, we could eat whatever they were eating—rice, soup, various vegetable dishes—and we did, sitting in an open-sided, thatched-roof hut, closely observed by a dog and a crow.

The atmosphere of this delightful enclave, where a steady trickle of communards dropped by to purchase groceries, reminded us of Auroville's namesake and guiding spirit, Sri Aurobindo, whose original ashram was founded in downtown Puducherry, in 1910, "not for the renunciation of the world but as a centre for the evolution of another form of life"—one, he wrote, that would "be moved by a higher spiritual consciousness."[6]

The ashram, like Auroville, was also flourishing, although after the 1973 death of Mirra Alfassa (known as the Mother), Sri Aurobindo's successor, the two communities came into conflict over issues of money and control. Now they were totally separate. The ashram's two thousand members were a force to be reckoned with in this pleasant provincial city. They operated an education centre, several health clinics, a publishing house and a number of cottage industries, which produced weaving, embroidery, batik, handmade paper and perfume. They also owned a great deal of property, including several inexpensive, spotless guest houses like the Park, where we stayed in a double room complete with a balcony overlooking the Indian Ocean.

At the main ashram building, which occupied an entire block, Indian and foreign devotees alike streamed into a lovely courtyard to pay their respects at the samadhi, or burial place, of Sri Aurobindo and the Mother. The tomb was tended daily by half a dozen women who arranged sweet-smelling petals and garlands of flowers over it in complex patterns. A great, spreading copperpod tree, covered with yellow flowers in late spring, dominated the space. Four evenings a week, an ethereal twenty-minute meditation, open to all, was held in the darkened courtyard, lit only by moonlight and the flicker of hundreds of sticks of incense.

Life at Auroville seemed more practical than at the ashram, which appeared to revolve around a cult-like celebration of its former leaders, but Auroville had its ethereal side as well. At its centre, for instance, a huge concrete bubble, which had been under construction for several decades, was slowly bursting out of the ground, signifying new life and the next step for humanity. This was the Matrimandir, a meeting and meditation space, and the heart of the community.

Not everyone in Auroville admired the Matrimandir. Many members would have preferred that the large sums spent on its construction went instead to more tangible, immediate projects. But there it stood. And if you were willing to endure a tedious ritual of waiting around, lining up single file and marching silently past scurrying workers along a circular ramp, you could peer for a few seconds into a white, pillared room at the top of the bubble. There, a glass sphere refracted light from a hole in the roof, illuminating the chamber in an otherworldly glow. It felt odd—quite a stretch, in fact—to come to this mystical place from the morning's biogas demonstration. But Auroville itself, we reflected, was quite a stretch: a strange and inspiring leap of the human imagination.

Speaking of the strange and inspiring, you may be wondering how Katherine and I were making out with our fragile new relationship. To be honest, I must admit that some cracks were appearing. We were still in the honeymoon phase, of course, but it was becoming obvious that work needed to be done. Travel in hot, humid India could be irritating as well as fascinating: think mosquitoes, bus and train delays, computer glitches, lineups and line crashers to start with. Things could get to you. When they got to me, I'd become surly and withdrawn, easily annoyed. My enthusiastic travelling companion crowded me, I felt, and her inevitable expectations pinned me down. My natural instinct was to blame India. But India wasn't going to change to suit me. I was the one who would have to change. There was no escape from each other here, as there would be at home, where we could back off to our respective corners from time to time. Here, we were yoked together like animals to a cart. Recognizing the problems and then being willing to talk about them were the only ways out.

In the meantime, spectacular religious centres waited to be explored. Some of India's oldest, largest temples were located in the state of Tamil Nadu, where Hinduism could be traced back four thousand years to the sophisticated culture of India's original inhabitants. These were the Dravidians, who migrated south in successive waves, and whose spiritual beliefs survived and flourished.

Foreign visitors were welcome to explore all but the innermost sanctums at most of these historic sites. Shoes (but not necessarily socks) had to be removed before entering and then left at one of the storage facilities found outside the temples; a receipt would usually be given, and your precious footwear well guarded. Travel bulletin: socks not widely available in southern India; bring extra pair from home.

To begin our temple tour we went by rail to Tiruchirappalli, or Trichy, a large city about two hundred kilometres southwest of Puducherry. Trichy was famous for its Rock Fort Temple, perched on a massive outcrop of smooth stone that erupted from the centre of town. Leading to the summit were 437 steps cut out of solid bedrock, a trek best made in the evening, when the air grew cooler as you climbed higher. From the peak, the old city was spread out at your feet, while the Cauvery River disappeared into the distance across a flat, fertile plain.

On an island in the river was the Ranganathaswamy or Srirangam Temple, ringed with seven concentric walls and entered via one of twenty-one multicoloured gopurams (gigantic towers covered top to bottom with images of supernatural beings). Few tourists visited this sixty-five-hectare complex, the largest functioning Hindu temple in the world. Priestly homes, food vendors and markets for household goods filled the spaces between the outer rings. You didn't have to surrender your shoes until the fourth wall, and beyond the seventh you could not pass. The temple was dedicated to the god Vishnu, and most pilgrims were Vaishnavites, his followers, their foreheads emblazoned with a vertical dash in an ochre V.

For a quieter and less congested view of religious architecture, we jumped on a bus to Thanjavur, or Tanjore, fifty-five kilometres east of Trichy. This small city was home to the magnificent Brihadisvara Temple, a UNESCO World Heritage Site and the showpiece of the Chola empire, whose rulers controlled much of southern Asia a millennium ago. It was still a place of worship. Groups of pilgrims—often men and children from the same rural village, all dressed in smart, identical pilgrimage lungis—would come up to us and try to converse. The language gap, unfortunately, was usually insurmountable, though smiles and friendly gestures could create a palpable sense of connection.

The gateway to Brihadisvara's inner courtyard was guarded by Nandi, Shiva's steed: an enormous bull carved from one piece of rock. Beyond it, the central shrine was capped by an eighty-one-tonne dome, also crafted from a single block of granite. The temple stonework was rich in detail; many pillars were inscribed with elegant Tamil script recording the names and feats of ancient benefactors.

Thousand-year-old frescoes adorned the walls and ceilings of the outer colonnades.

As we left Brihadisvara, an elephant waited patiently in the shade of the main gopuram, its great ears and leathery tail flicking away the ever-present insects. We were headed south from here to unknown territory and new adventures; a blessing seemed in order. I tentatively held out a rupee, which the elephant took with a surprising, delicate movement of its trunk and passed to its minder, or mahout. Then it placed the tip of its trunk, which was pink and quite moist, on my balding head in the equivalent of an elephant kiss. Thus sanctified, I proceeded on my way.

In the large southern Indian city of Madurai, the streets leading to Meenakshi Temple throbbed with beeping scooters and autorickshaws. Sidewalk tailors worked away at sewing machines, while shopkeepers did a thriving trade in lottery tickets and bicycle parts. Cows and dogs wandered in search of food or else slept in the road.

We were headed to Meenakshi to see the evening closing ceremony. A palanquin bearing an image of Shiva would be carried with great ceremony to the sleeping quarters of his consort, the divine Parvati. Drummers, horn blowers, torchbearers and fan-waving attendants helped put the god to bed each night, after which the temple gates were locked. In a side shrine, I saw my elephant friend, Ganesh, the god of wisdom and prosperity, and a much-loved Hindu deity. He was Shiva and Parvati's son.

The temple dated from only the sixteenth century, but it had such a magnetic pull on the city that one tended to forget that Madurai, a bustling centre with a population of a million and a half, had itself been a vital centre of learning and pilgrimage for more than two thousand years. Every day, tens of thousands of devotees were attracted there. Most wore three horizontal chalk lines on their foreheads to indicate that they were Shaivites, followers of Shiva. The Hindu pantheon of gods could be confusing for westerners, but the three main figures—Brahma the creator, Vishnu the preserver and Shiva the destroyer and transformer—could be seen as different aspects of one omnipresent god.

As we wandered Meenakshi's inner corridors, we realized that solemnity and silence were as out of place here as belly dancing would be in Canterbury Cathedral. Flower garlands, incense and pictures of gods and goddesses were on noisy sale. Worshippers gathered to talk on steps leading down to the Golden Lotus Tank, a large pond. In the evenings, musicians performed on squeezebox, stringed instruments, tabla drums and bells, and the music was piped throughout the temple.

In the shadowy Hall of a Thousand Pillars (really there were only 985, all beautifully carved and supporting a vividly painted ceiling), visitors strolled and chatted. The atmosphere was casual. University students engaged us in polite, formal conversation, while tip-seeking priests offered temple tours. A shy young couple with a small child, their scalps shaved bald and painted in yellow ochre, wanted us to share their modest meal.

As we headed back to the hotel in the fading light, a temple elephant, its day's work almost done, stopped beside us so a passerby could receive a benediction. Old hands by now, we confidently held out coins as well. Ganesh tapped our heads, the mahout wished us well, and we felt ready for the next stage of our journey.

Things started to fall apart on the bus trip from Kodaikanal, a hill station northwest of Madurai. The weather had been cool and wet, and we didn't have the right clothing. The much-vaunted panoramic views were hidden by cloud. The museum was closed, as were the best gardens; walking was about it for entertainment. My journal notes degenerated into a litany of complaints: not enough hot water at the hotel, inadequate reading lamps, extra charges for toilet paper and an upper sheet. I grew paranoid, convinced the room was deliberately underfurnished so that hotel employees could bring us stuff we needed and cadge tips. The restaurant staff stared at me so intently that they neglected their duties. Did I sound like a fun guy to travel with?

Katherine didn't think so. "I'm just finding it very difficult to deal with your irritability and anger," she said, delicately. "It seems to be happening more and more, almost all the time."

At first I was surprised. What anger?

"Well, just now, for instance, when the water bottle leaked on the seat, just a few drops, you got pissed off right away. And when the men in front of us started smoking.

And when the restaurant was closed this morning when we went for lunch. 'Fuck,' you said. You always swear and get all exasperated and negative. I mean, this is India, and things are going to go wrong all the time. We'll never make it travelling together at this rate."

I sat quietly and observed my reaction to her comments. Yes, here it came, a stab of red-hot outrage. I was a fool to think this arrangement would work out. Then came a wave of self-pity. Something always went wrong when I took the initiative. Only a short step to bitterness now. To hell with everything and everyone. Neither of us spoke. The bus jounced down the steep road: jungle and rock out one window, sheer precipice on the other side. It was a long fall to the flat farmlands below. I fell into a daze.

And then I saw him. Right there in the bus. Someone else was travelling with me. Someone else always had been. He was a family retainer, of sorts. A dark shadow. I had long been aware, of course, of his presence, but I could never see him clearly. As soon as the spotlight of consciousness shone in his direction, he'd flit away. But today, perhaps because of the unfamiliar surroundings and our unusual activities, he had been caught out in the open. For once I had a plain view of him.

He was a disappointed man, was the shadow. He had a frown or scowl that kept people away. He was a wet blanket, living in expectation of some future fulfillment. I asked him who he was and where he came from. He was oriented in time, not space. Instead of east and west, he knew only past and future. He pointed a skinny finger behind him, and

I glimpsed a desolate landscape, littered with abandoned expectations and derailed intentions.

The shadow's role was to maintain this pattern, to keep it intact and viable. Why, you could sabotage everything, I realized, as long as I lived. He grinned eagerly. If I let you. He looked confused. You are not me, I said, only part of me. The shadow had nowhere to go. I'll make you a deal, I said. You can travel with me but you cannot drive the bus. He hung his head.

I turned to Katherine. I told her about the shadow. Sounds familiar, she laughed. She had djinn of her own. Perhaps we could remind each other, I thought—help each other see what we had temporarily become. By the time we were back on the steaming Deccan Plateau, the scenes around us had returned to some degree of normalcy. I felt ready to resume the journey, knowing that my capacity for wonder would be tested many times in the weeks to come.

We continued north by train, our goal being Hospet, a small city from which we could explore the magical ruins of Hampi, another UNESCO World Heritage Site (India has thirty-eight). En route we felt compelled to stop at Mysore (Mysuru), or Sandalwood City, India's beautiful incense and perfume capital, where we splurged on accommodation and stayed at the Hotel Metropole, once the guest house of the maharaja. The palace, with its splendid domes and arches and colonnades, dominated the city centre and winked knowingly at much older Islamic and Saracenic designs but was not, in itself, very old at all. Nor was it very Asian. It had been conceived by an Irish architect, Henry Irwin, in 1897, in the Indo-Gothic style (one might call it "tropical colonial") preferred during the era of the British Raj, that century and a half of foreign sovereignty that didn't end until 1947.

Hampi, however, was the real thing: one of the country's great archaeological destinations. In the fifteenth and sixteenth centuries, as the capital of southern India's Vijayanagara Empire, Hampi had the distinction of being the second-largest city on the planet (after Beijing). Its royal palaces, temples and shrines were spread over a hilly, forty-square-kilometre area strewn with boulders and low-growing shrubs. We particularly enjoyed the king's elephant stables, with their gigantic entryways and elaborate inscriptions. There were commercial and residential ruins, as well: an arena, marketplaces, roads, an aqueduct, water tanks, bathhouses. About sixteen hundred monuments could be visited.

We had the ancient city more or less to ourselves—inevitable, really, considering its size. It was easy to get lost there, and that, of course, is what we immediately proceeded to do. There were few signs and no maps, and somewhere near the Hazara Ramachandra Temple, with its fantastic frescoes of Hindu festivals and its scenes from the Ramayana, we wandered off the beaten track. Many hours later I had to pay a boy several rupees to lead us out to a road and point the way to a bus stop.

By this point in our journey we were getting tired of temples and ruins and long bus journeys, and were looking forward to Christmas on the beach. Each morning, over breakfast, we'd find a daily newspaper in English and review the previous day's industrial accidents and highway carnage, feeling both relief that we were still alive and horror that so many innocent people had met such terrible fates. We had sworn to take no more bus rides longer than four hours but felt that we could endure a final train journey, from Hospet to Goa on the west coast. Then we discovered that extensive track repairs were underway and there was no train to Goa. Only the dreaded bus was available (Hospet had no airport). We were stuck. No choice. The bus conductor proudly ushered us to reserved seats right behind the driver, with a fine view out the windshield. The next ten hours were spent flinching, cringing and cowering as our driver gambled with death, overtaking on blind corners, driving on the wrong side of the road, narrowly dodging pedestrians, and crushing farmyard animals.

By the time we reached our destination, we were so wasted we were barely able to move. 'Twas the season to be jolly in Goa, but we were unable to rise to the occasion. There was no room at the inn—not at the first inn, nor the second, nor even the sixth. Our terrible bus journey, plus another hour searching for a place to sleep in the tiny beachside village of Benaulim, had left us somewhat frayed. With mighty forbearance, one of us refrained from saying "I told you so" to the other. It was mid-December, a time when accommodations were best booked in advance. We hadn't.

At 10:00 p.m., our taxi tentatively bumped down a dark lane, and the headlights came to rest on a small guest house shrouded by tropical trees: our last hope. The one who had failed to book in advance (despite the urgings of the other) entered the home with instructions to accept whatever was available, providing it included a bed.

"I said we'd take it," was the report, "but they have to remove the rice first." From the taxi we could see beyond the entry hall into a minute bedroom where members of the owner's family were scooping mounds of drying rice into baskets. Our hosts had volunteered to sleep with it tonight.

"Basic" is how the young English backpackers we'd met on the bus had described this typical Goan guest house. They were staying there, in a spacious, rice-free room, because they had wisely booked ahead, knowing that at Christmas Goa was inundated with throngs of Europeans on cheap charters and Indians from Mumbai, four hundred kilometres north. It was also a mecca for travellers like ourselves, seeking a place to unwind after the rigours of exploring India. Seductive beaches, sunshine and unspoiled tropical scenery were the attractions. Throw in great seafood, friendly inhabitants and dirt-cheap prices and it wasn't surprising that a lively travellers' scene had grown up along Goa's hundred-kilometre coastline. Popular year-round, India's smallest state reached its busy peak during the holiday season.

Goa came within Portugal's acquisitive grasp in 1510, when it was captured by Afonso de Albuquerque. Thirty years later, Francis Xavier arrived in the new colony to promote Christianity. The Portuguese relinquished control of Goa only in 1961, fourteen years after Indian independence. They left a fine legacy of colonial architecture, especially in Old Goa, where Saint Francis Xavier's mummified remains could be seen in one of the town's enormous churches. This Iberian influence had created for Goans a reputation for being more indulgent and easygoing than Indians in the rest of the country.

Before joining the Goans in their tropical languor, visitors first had to decide which palm-fringed stretch of sand and associated village would be their temporary home. We settled on Benaulim, described in our guidebook as one of the more tranquil spots along Goa's sunset-facing coastline. Not for us the rave beaches like Calangute and Anjuna, where dope-smoking hedonists had held sway since the 1960s.

Benaulim village, we discovered after leaving our guest house the next morning, was just a few shops, a tiny church and a bus stop. No five-star or even five-storey hotels were available, though construction in the area suggested that the village's rural nature might soon come under threat. We rented bicycles to conduct a search for more upscale digs than the rice room. Each of us had harboured a vision of a beachside cottage set in dense greenery, a vision that grew more remote by the minute. The garish, spanking-new building on Benaulim's main road was not even close to our fantasies. But when the friendly owner showed us a quiet corner room with a balcony, we heaved a collective sigh of relief and slapped down a deposit. "We have twenty-four-hour hot-water shower and we are fixing the fan," said Jacinta, the ever-cheerful chambermaid.

Within days, we had a well-established routine: sunning, swimming and feasting. It was the perfect antidote to last month's trains, temples and buses. At low tide, we collected shells and cycled for hours along the firm, clean sands, sometimes to neighbouring villages, sometimes until a lagoon finally blocked our way.

Signs of Christmas appeared soon after our arrival. Porches were hung with illuminated paper stars. Huge ornaments of rattan and paper were displayed on prominent street corners. Tinsel, paper ribbons and coloured lights snaked round live Norfolk pines and other plants. Many front yards featured charming homemade nativity scenes. The local dance hall was decked with red and green flashing lights.

Those with an urge to buy Christmas presents could shop on the beach, where a brigade of relentless vendors patrolled all year, selling mats, hats, shirts, drums, tablecloths, carved elephants and saffron, or else offering massages and henna treatments. "Just looking, sir, just looking," they would plead if you feigned indifference.

For extreme seasonal shopping, the labyrinthine market at Anjuna beckoned, sandwiched between sea and rice paddies forty-five kilometres north of Benaulim. On the last market day before Christmas, a thousand visitors forsook their various beach resorts to jostle one another at this weekly bazaar, where Tibetan, Indian, European and North American vendors flogged silk paintings, silver jewellery, hash pipes, crystals, spices, wood carvings and Kashmiri painted boxes.

Upon arrival, we were assaulted by a man brandishing a lethal-looking pointed instrument, who pantomimed his eagerness to clean our ears. A turbaned old-timer blew tunelessly into a flute as he paraded a festooned, painted, bell-ringing cow. A sign on an incongruous canvas teepee advertised body piercing and tattoos. Those seeking less dangerous ways to spend their rupees could get a haircut or a shoeshine.

The fair was a kaleidoscope of colour. Silk and cotton clothing and wall hangings floated from ropes strung between palms. Gujarati women wearing elaborate costumes, silver bangles, ear and nose rings and necklaces aggressively urged us to examine their goods. "Come see my shop, madam. What you pay?"

We departed Anjuna with our purchases—a colourful sarong and a silk elephant print to be exchanged later as Christmas presents—and retreated to bucolic Benaulim. Over the next few days, Goa's holiday pace gathered steam, especially at the restaurants, which outdid each other with all-you-can-eat buffets, beach barbecues and fireworks displays. On Christmas Day, serenaded by a motley crew of carollers, we celebrated at our favourite dining spot, a simple shack far down the beach, with grilled salmon, prawn fried rice, vegetable curry, beer and banana crepes for dessert.

A week later, at New Year's, we saw a colourful tent, or shamiana, being raised on Benaulim Beach for the evening's live-band dance. We were here to recuperate, not to party, so we opted for another seafood banquet and a quiet evening. Heading for breakfast the next morning, we met the last of the night's revellers staggering off to bed. We may have missed a little excitement, but we got an excellent start to another year. We made our resolutions: one of us promised to continue practising forbearance, while the other—for Christmas, at least—made up his mind to book ahead.

The Goa section of the India chapter is based on newspaper articles that Katherine and Andrew wrote, jointly and separately, in the late 1990s.

South Korea 1998

The evening before we travelled through the Hallyeo Waterway, I went for an extravagant seafood meal with my guide James and his friends Mr. Kim and Mr. Lee. We drank lots of beer. Then we took a long taxi ride to a distant suburb and a subterranean honeycomb of karaoke rooms called the Music Box. We drank more beer. At one point I was astonished to find myself singing "Imagine" and "Solitary Man" to a roomful of strangers. We apparently joined up with another Mr. Kim, whose car sped us later to Utopia, a swank nightclub.

Here Mr. Lee and the several Messrs. Kim, still refusing any contribution to what was rapidly turning into a very expensive evening, had me out on the dance floor until the wee hours, whirling in curious Asian free-for-all style with an energetic crowd of local celebrants. It was a fine introduction to the boisterous, sprawling seaport of Pusan, and a characteristic instance of South Korean generosity. If I hadn't remembered to politely decline the *soju*, a distilled liquor much loved by the country's serious drinkers, I'd have missed the boat for sure.

That would have been inconvenient. The main reason for my presence on Korea's southern coast in December was

A waterfront scene at the seaport of Yeosu, in South Korea.

to make the notable, two-hundred-kilometre ferry trip from Pusan to Yeosu. So there I was at 7:00 a.m., up on the roof of the Pusan ferry terminal, groggily taking photographs of the busy, crowded harbour and watching the early morning boats weave through the traffic of tankers, tenders and tugs on their way to outlying fishing ports and island towns.

South Korea had become one of the world's leading maritime nations, and Pusan was a vibrant expression of the country's ocean-going spirit. From there you could take a giant car ferry to the semi-tropical volcanic island of Jeju, where honeymooners flocked, or book passenger vessels to Shimonoseki and Osaka in southern Japan. But if you wanted to journey comfortably through the region's protected inland waters, then the Angel hydrofoil was the craft you'd be looking for.

The twenty-one-metre-long Angels, built in the 1980s by the giant Korean conglomerate Hyundai, were powerful pieces of machinery: their 1,350-horsepower, single-prop engines could push them along at speeds of more than forty knots (seventy-five kilometres per hour). About one hundred passengers could be seated, aircraft-style, by a crew of four, smartly uniformed in green windbreakers and black slacks. Our boat, *Angel 10,* was only one-third full. We preferred the seats above the engine, located amidships; they had the best view because they were higher.

We had arranged to break our journey and stay overnight at the pleasant port city of Chungmu (now part of Tongyeong). It took only two hours to get there, including stops at the industrial ship-building town of Seongpo and at a small fishing village on Koje Island. The hydrofoil shared the Hallyeo Waterway with hundreds of trawlers and freighters and skirted dozens of mariculture operations, usually oyster farms with neat rows of white polystyrene floats beneath which the juvenile shellfish were raised.

As the rocky headlands glided past, and the first of the area's four hundred forested, evergreen islands started to come into view, I felt we might easily have been cruising along Canada's west coast, where I lived. I spent so much time on islands and ferries at home that you would think I'd seek out something different when travelling abroad: deserts, for instance, or mountaintops or icefields. But perhaps we are always attracted to a type of landscape that is familiar and well loved, even in unfamiliar places.

Unfamiliar scenes soon began to appear—sights that Vancouverites would have to travel a long way to view. Fallow rice paddies occupied many lower elevations along our route, and racks of squid, a favourite Korean delicacy, could be seen in the villages, drying in the sun. History raised its head, as well. Nowhere in British Columbia, for instance, was the present so dominated by a single character from the past. For me, the next few days would be marked by the ghostly presence of Admiral Yi Sun-shin, a sixteenth-century action figure who seemed to embody the spirit of the region.

Even the name of the town to which we were headed reflected Admiral Yi's glory: Chungmu meant "loyalty" and "military valour" and was taken from a title conferred posthumously on the famed warrior. A naval command centre was established there in 1604 following more than a decade of warfare between Korea and Japan. Although Korea was eventually overrun by the Japanese army, its naval forces, under Yi's command, won a series of major showdowns against vastly larger fleets, and the admiral passed into legend as an unparalleled military strategist and innovator. There were tributes to him everywhere along this stretch of coast.

After arriving in Chungmu and consuming steaming bowls of fish soup in a tiny restaurant, James and I took a long, narrow tourist boat out to Hallyeohaesang National Park, which protected more than five hundred square kilometres of coves and inlets, cliffs and beaches, between Pusan and Yeosu. In summer, these boats would be bulging with Korean vacationers, down south for the swimming, fishing, diving and water skiing, but today we were only eight: a formally attired honeymooning couple, a young American-born investment banker of Korean heritage visiting his ancestral home for the first time, a Pusan university student with relatives in Chungmu, James and myself, and the crew.

Our destination was Haegeumgang, a camellia-smothered outcropping off the southern tip of Koje Island. There were lots of spectacular rock formations in this area, and the captain announced them on a loudspeaker as we passed: Dukkobi-bawi (Toad Rock), Saja-bawi (Lion Rock), Sonnyo-bawi (Nymph Rock), Haegol-bawi (Skeleton Rock), Tugu-bawi (Helmet Rock) and the most remarkable of them all, Chotte-bawi (Candlestick Rock), a slender pinnacle carved by wind and ocean.

We dutifully admired these monuments before arriving at the black, ominous entrance to Sipja Donggul, the Cross-Shaped Cave. Appropriately, the captain had a surprise in store for those of us who didn't understand Korean and thus were not up to date on the afternoon's activities: he intended to take his boat *into* the cave. As the cave mouth was less than a metre wider than the boat, and large waves were crashing on all the surrounding rocks, this didn't seem like a good idea to me. But he went ahead and did it anyway. The deckhand scurried from side to side adjusting the fenders in case of a crash, but they weren't needed. So delicate was the captain's touch that we never even grazed the rock walls, which rose above us into the bat-filled darkness like a primitive temple. Later, we checked out several other caves and arches in the cliffs, much to the delight of a group of grinning fishermen, who gave us a cheer as we backed narrowly out of Olum-gul, the Ice Cave.

Following these thrills, the return to Chungmu was anticlimactic. We collected our bags and patrolled the waterfront streets in search of a *yogwan*, or traditional Korean inn. These are handily identified, for foreigners at least, by a "hot springs" symbol—an oval representing a tub, with vertical lines coming out of it to signify rising heat; yogwans were originally built beside these natural bathing spots. Our simple rooms had heated floors, or *ondol*, which we were grateful for as it was winter and the mild daytime temperatures plummeted at night.

That evening we wandered through the market and looked in the shops. Every kind of seafood was being sold: alive, recently alive, shrivelled and desiccated, or cooked and ready to eat. At a distance, the different types of dried fish resembled a hardware display, arrayed in boxes like a sequence of silvery nails, bolts and rivets. Their pungent odour filled the air. Ruddy-faced women in baggy clothes pleaded with us to buy a kind of big, red, pot-bellied cod, rows of which were laid out on the sidewalk along with all sorts of fresh and dried seaweeds and piles of gourds, pumpkins and persimmons. Breads and cakes beckoned from dozens of European-style bakeries. But, tired and still slightly hungover, we passed these delights by and opted for an early night.

The next morning, I roamed the docks, watching the catch being rapidly sorted out and distributed. The dockside fishing boats were marked on either side of their bows with painted eyes, to help the fishermen find their prey. That day they had been successful. A torrent of pewter-coloured eels and small, red-brown lampreys were being boxed and bagged, destined for restaurants and fish stalls. I crossed the bridge that connected downtown Chungmu to Miruk Island and returned via a pedestrian underwater tunnel, built in 1931 by the Japanese during their most recent occupation.

After breakfast we caught a shuttle boat to Hansan Island, where the Chesungdang shrine preserved a complex of exquisite pavilions, courtyards and gates on the site of Admiral Yi's 1592 headquarters. It had rained heavily the night before, but as we approached Hansan the sky cleared and the sun picked out a gleaming white navigation beacon built in the shape of one of Yi's notorious turtle ships. These early ironclad vessels, designed to mimic the shell of a turtle, proved an effective equalizer in the admiral's uneven battles with the Japanese. At Chesungdang, maps show how Yi enticed the Japanese fleet into a narrow channel next to Hansan, surrounded it with his own ships, then destroyed or captured most of the enemy craft. His shrine was a beautiful, peaceful spot, framed with graceful maple and pine trees. Signs enjoined visitors to "worship with a pious mind."

Soon it was time to continue our journey. On sunny days it was a good idea to take the afternoon hydrofoil, as you were likely to find yourself travelling through an extraordinary sunset. We made stops at a picturesque village on tiny Saryang Island, at a port on the east coast of the large island of Namhae and at the sizable mainland town of Samcheonpo, which was engaged in a delicate environmental juggling act: on one side, it sported a gigantic coal-fired power plant; on the other, an islet sanctuary for South Korea's rare white herons.

Our two-hour ferry ride behind us, we slipped smoothly into Yeosu, another appealing seaport, larger than Chungmu but similar in atmosphere, and also connected by an impressive bridge to an adjacent island. According to my guide, the people of Yeosu had a reputation for unfriendliness, but I found them likeable, with a rough and ready manner; the women in particular were robust and quite striking in appearance, and looked you straight in the eye. In fact, more people came up and talked to me here on my early morning waterfront rambles than anywhere else in Korea.

One older gentleman, elegantly attired in suit and greatcoat, was surprised to meet a westerner in Yeosu in winter. We chatted for a few minutes and then he stepped carefully aboard a rustbucket of a local ferry and was soon on his way to who knows where. Another fellow, a teacher, out for a jog and wearing a track suit, offered to take me to see Chinju, a nearby town of great historic interest, site of a fourteenth-century castle. I wished I'd had time to accept, and also to visit Namhae Island, rich in natural beauty and shrines commemorating Admiral Yi.

James and I whiled away our remaining hours on the south coast at Odong, a tiny island park, connected to the mainland by a causeway and carpeted with camellias and rhododendrons. There we watched Yeosu's women divers, suited head to toe in black neoprene, brave the frigid waters to gather shellfish for Odong's famous seafood restaurants. Admiral Yi had been to Odong, too. It was there that his troops collected an unusually hard and straight-growing variety of bamboo for use as arrows. Back in downtown Yeosu, the Chinnamgwan pavilion, a lovely old building with massive posts and beams, sheltered two full-scale models of the turtle ships.

Before heading to the airport for our flight to Seoul, we climbed high up on a hill overlooking the city, where yet another three-hundred-year-old shrine, Chungmin-sa, extolled the virtues of the heroic Yi. His statue stood staring out to sea, as if in search of his next adventure. I stood beside him to search for mine, looking west to where another huge national park, Dadohae Haesang, began. Complete with seaports and fishing villages and ferries, Dadohae encompassed hundreds more of South Korea's thirty-three hundred islands—enough strange but familiar landscapes to keep a coast-loving traveller coming back again and again.

Vietnam 2002

A chirpy voice hailed us as we pedalled through the lush, pastoral landscape of rice paddies and waterways. "Are you Canadians? I heard someone say there were Canadians." A tiny, birdlike Vietnamese woman, also on a bicycle, caught up and started firing questions at us in English. What part of Canada were we from? What kind of work did we do? Why did we come to Vietnam?

Canadians were good to talk to, she claimed: easygoing, broad-minded. In fact, we were thrilled to have a conversation with an actual Mekong Delta resident. Minh had studied English as a trainee teacher, improved her language skills on the tourists and worked at a primary school nearby. We wheeled our bikes together over the graceful arch of a footbridge. "This is my favourite spot," Minh said, fluttering her hand at the flat green delta that scrolled away to the horizon. "From here you can see all the islands." Palms and mango trees lined the canals, where narrow wooden riverboats were tethered. Bright bougainvillea cascaded over fences and walls. "This is my whole world," she sighed.

Her words threw into relief the differences between us. The farthest Minh had been from home was sweltering Ho Chi Minh City, eighty kilometres away, where we

The Hindu ruins of Po Nagar, near Nha Trang in Vietnam, have been repurposed as a Buddhist monument.

had landed three days before. By contrast, Katherine and I would travel the sixteen-hundred-kilometre length of this sultry Southeast Asian country, from south to north, in the single month of April. This was Katherine's first visit, but I had been here eight years before. Inspired by the friendliness and serenity of the long-suffering Vietnamese, I vowed to return to see how their war-scrambled country's cautious opening to the wider world might unfold.

About Ho Chi Minh City (or Saigon), Vietnam's largest metropolis—home to seven million people and three million motor scooters—we found ourselves in complete agreement with Minh: great neighbourhoods, fascinating museums and markets, unbelievable food, can't wait to leave. Nevertheless, we spent an obligatory couple of days exploring the city, seeing first-hand those places made famous by footage from the Vietnam War: the Rex Hotel, where the US military command gave its daily press briefings; the elegant City Hall or Hôtel de Ville; the Saigon Opera House; Gia Long Palace, former home of the Supreme Court and now the Ho Chi Minh City Museum; Notre-Dame Cathedral; and the site of the US embassy (demolished in 1998) with its famous rooftop helipad.

Best of all were the Reunification Palace and the War Remnants Museum. The palace, with its underground network of tunnels and command stations, was where South Vietnam's president and vice-president had lived, with their families. The gruesome photo exhibits at the museum told the story of the Vietnam War from the victors' point of view. A nifty selection of captured military hardware was also on display: tanks, flame-throwing vehicles, armoured bulldozers, warplanes and a helicopter, plus lots of guns, of course.

The need to escape the noise and congestion of Saigon soon reached the imperative stage, and we boarded an open-sided riverboat, along with a handful of other travellers, for a tour around the Mekong Delta. The delta was the nation's rice bowl and beating rural heart, so fertile and productive that Vietnam had become the world's second-largest exporter of rice, after Thailand.

Travelling by boat, we learned, was a far more relaxed way to see the country than riding a bus. Buses were accident-prone and broke down regularly. Roads were overcrowded and seemed always under repair. (We'd often see little groups of forlorn passengers waiting patiently at the side of the road while mechanics performed major surgery on their vehicle.) A bewildering variety of vessels cruised the canals that criss-crossed the delta: wooden dugouts, small passenger craft with long propeller shafts designed for manoeuvring in shallows, great plodding sand barges with families in aft cabins making dinner or drying laundry. Most boats sported red-and-white eyes painted on the bows to ward off evil spirits.

There were boats carrying sugar cane, banana leaves, rice (of course), bricks, used cardboard for recycling, cases of beer and cans of cooking oil. Some folk waved and smiled; others ignored us. Our heads swivelled like weather vanes; we hardly knew what to look at next. When traffic slowed, we turned our attention to the banks, where naked children cannonballed from houses on pilings into the murky, coffee-coloured canals. Small-scale commerce—from basket weaving to coffin making—flourished. Hectares of seedlings and bedding plants were set out on platforms above the water.

Over the course of the tour we stopped to visit several businesses: a family operation where rice was puffed and baked into cakes, another minifactory where rice wraps for spring rolls were produced, a large rice mill, two different catfish farms, a coconut-candy manufacturer and an incense maker. There were no gift shops or sales pitches, just giggles and timid smiles. Our guide, Nghia, explained the processes and translated our questions.

We met Minh the first day out. To our surprise, she told us that she and her family were Catholics. Indeed, a small Christian church stood beside the watery intersection where we paused to enjoy the view. We would have liked to discuss all manner of things with Minh, especially the great mix of religions found in the delta: Buddhism, Christianity, Hinduism, Islam and Caodaism. This last sect, with five million adherents, mostly in southern Vietnam, intrigued us especially. Founded in 1926, it placed a heavy emphasis on spiritualism and venerated the French author Victor Hugo, the Chinese statesman Sun Yat-sen and the sixteenth-century Vietnamese poet Nguyen Binh Khiem as major prophets. I'd attended a service at its highly ornate (think Tiger Balm Gardens) main temple in Tay Ninh on my last trip. Hundreds of priests and priestesses, dressed in white, red, yellow and blue robes, and wearing various highly decorative hats, had filed into the temple and chanted and prayed to the accompaniment of a live orchestra.

But, alas, our boat's departure time drew near. Sadly, we said goodbye to Minh and returned our bikes to the restaurant we had rented them from. Back aboard, we emerged shortly from the network of canals into the mighty Mekong itself. Its Vietnamese name was Song Cuu Long, or River of Nine Dragons—a reference to the Mekong's nine branches. The dragon we slew first, crossing to the large town of Vinh Long, was Tien Giang, or the Upper River. From there we took a short bus ride to another boat, which braved the Bassac or Lower River to arrive at the pleasant city of Can Tho, hub of the delta. Dusk found us eating grilled fish and spicy eggplant at a converted villa overlooking the water.

Early the next morning was floating-market time. We raced downriver to Cai Rang, where our skipper hurled his boat into a bouncing, jostling melee, a maritime version of bumper cars. Wholesalers displayed their wares on poles. Retailers clustered round, bargaining fiercely. Loud vendors hawked food, drink and souvenirs. Tourists got in the way. An hour of this and we clambered aboard a boat selling *trái khóm*, or pineapples. The owners quickly trimmed a dozen specimens, and we ate the sweet, delicious fruit whole, like corn on the cob.

Later we transferred to a larger riverboat, which travelled all afternoon to Chau Doc, a town on the Cambodian border. Some of our group would continue up the Bassac the following morning to Phnom Penh, Cambodia's capital.

The rest of us investigated cave temples and a Muslim village where vivid sarongs were woven. We travelled in tiny, tippy, open craft rowed by laughing women who perched at the stern and pushed on their oars from a standing position. Then it was back to the riverboat for a downstream rendezvous with the dreaded bus and a return to Ho Chi Minh City.

When I first visited Vietnam, in 1994, its Communist leaders were still very suspicious of the wicked West. Tourism was in its infancy; most hotels were crude, and travel was primitive and punishing. Vietnam's terrible war had put the country decades behind the rest of the world. By default I was getting a glimpse of an older, more traditional Asia: rural, agricultural, with a pace of life geared to pedestrians, bicycles, ox carts and very slow, decrepit trains. This was all that Vietnam could show visitors, because this was all Vietnam had.

On my second visit, almost a decade later, I found that many aspects of Vietnam—the superb cuisine, the beach and mountain scenery, the temples and ruins, the openness and optimism of the people—were much the same. Travel was still exhausting, and the train remained excruciatingly slow. But the signs of war had receded. Tourism was booming now. All hotel rooms had—gasp—hot water. Construction was rampant. So were pollution, noise and traffic congestion. Vietnam's spirit was as strong as ever, but its eighty million residents, packed into a long, narrow country the size of Norway, and bounded by Cambodia, Laos and China, were paying a heavy price for development.

Tourist buses, unheard of my first time around, were ubiquitous, and we took one to Nha Trang, our next destination, a mid-sized city on the southern coast. It was a twelve-hour ride, but the bus was fairly new, with air conditioning, and the first half of the journey was uneventful, despite the incessant honking. We broke for lunch at Mui Ne, a pretty coastal village with fine beaches and a scattering of hotels. We should have stayed there. When our vehicle finally returned after a long delay, the air-con was no longer working. Neither were the lights, which meant that the bus had to be driven at breakneck speed in order to reach Nha Trang before dark. Worst of all, the horn had been silenced, which greatly pleased the passengers but seemed to enrage the driver and prompt him to psychotic bouts of overtaking.

Bound by a splendid municipal beach, Nha Trang proved a good place to recover from our ordeal. In Vietnam, we discovered, most visitors needed a frequent refuge from the overwhelming pace of everyday life. Vehicular travel could be especially stressful. We swung in hammocks on our hotel's roof terrace and considered our options. Option one—exploration by boat, rail and bike when possible, plus the occasional cheap and painless flight—received two votes. Option two—numerous bus journeys of six hours and longer—received no votes at all. It was democracy in action, and reason to celebrate with sour fish soup and tamarind sauce at a nearby restaurant.

Bicycle travel, surprisingly, was less dangerous than one

might imagine. Even traffic on Highway 1, the Trans-Vietnamese Obstacle Course, had a definite pattern; once you found your place between the scooters and the pedestrians at the edge of the thick torrent of trucks, buses and farm vehicles, you could roll along in relative safety. But if you stopped or changed direction suddenly, you risked throwing the entire elaborate system into chaos and causing an accident. The main Vietnamese rule of the road was "Biggest goes first," and tourists on bicycles needed to make that their mantra.

First we pedalled out to Po Nagar near Nha Trang to see traces of the once great Hindu empire of Champa. The crumbling, eighth-century, red brick towers had been repurposed as Buddhist monuments; now they were a hive of activity for monks, nuns, beggars, vendors and tourists. At Hoi An and Hue on the central coast we made long, idyllic outings by bike into a peaceful countryside, where friendly farmers tended rice paddies and water buffalo roamed.

For a longer excursion, to My Son, the most extensive of Vietnam's Cham ruins, we took a bus from Hoi An. The road was as bad as it had been nine years ago, when I travelled this way on a rented motor scooter, but at least there were no road-closure scams and fake "official" entry booths, as there had been in 1994. These local initiatives, designed to extract money from unwary tourists, attempted to fool people into taking a primitive ferry across a river when, a bit farther on, there was a footbridge.

My Son's wild, rugged setting, overlooked by Cat's Tooth Mountain (Hon Quap), made the inconvenience of the journey worthwhile. There were no signs of modern civilization at the site, just the remains of sixty-eight religious monuments, five of which had been flattened by American bombers during the Vietnam War (or American War, as the Vietnamese called it). Twenty were still standing, remarkably intact.

Here was Champa's main cultural centre, and the burial place of its monarchs, who ruled much of southern Vietnam from about AD 200 to 1600. I'd never even heard of the Chams until I first visited Vietnam; the name mocked my pretensions as a traveller. With their Sanskrit inscriptions and fine carvings of elephants, bulls and six-armed Shiva figures, the monuments seemed like Indian outposts lost in an Oriental landscape. With the help of Italy, two *mandapas* or meditation halls had been converted to small, open-air museums, where visitors could look through grilles at stone and brick sculptures found at the site. Little other restoration had been done, and some splendid jungle threatened to reclaim many of the ruins.

Vísitors could tromp through that jungle, if they liked, to see more heavily damaged structures. I passed on this option. My Son was a Viet Cong base during the war—which is why the Americans bombed it—and the area was heavily mined. In 1977, six Vietnamese sappers had died here during clearing operations. Even today, grazing cows were sometimes blown up. Just wandering around the beaten paths and breathing in the pure, history-laden air was enough for me.

Hoi An was everyone's favourite refuge in Vietnam: a charming seventeenth-century trading port that had miraculously escaped destruction in the American War. The twenty-first-century trade was mostly in custom-made clothing. Tailors had taken the town over, and travellers stocked up on everything from scarves to suits, all of which could be finished in a matter of hours. In central Hoi An, homes, storefronts and pagodas had been restored and turned into beautiful restaurants, galleries and museums. Courtyard gardens were framed invitingly through doorways. At night we sat at candlelit, open-air restaurants and tried the local delicacies: saffron tuna grilled in banana leaf, fried won ton and *cao lau*, a dish of noodles, bean sprouts and pork mixed with crumbled rice paper. Lanterns turned the waterfront and narrow streets into romantic kingdoms of colour.

We took a number of journeys by water. A converted fishboat ferried us to a group of offshore islands, where we snorkelled, watched sea eagles swoop and dive, and waded through a superb buffet lunch. Fishing villagers paddled us about in tiny "basket boats"—bowl-shaped dinghies woven from rattan and sealed with pitch. At Hue, where Vietnam's emperors had held sway in the eighteenth and nineteenth centuries, we floated down the Perfume River to the manicured, pleasure-garden burial sites of the imperial rulers.

Everywhere we went we met Viet Kieu, or overseas Vietnamese, usually young Americans back to visit relatives, meet potential spouses and tour their ancestral homeland.

They moved with confidence among their poorer cousins and seemed to us like modern aristocrats: the emperors and empresses of the new Vietnam. Neither they nor any resident Vietnamese we talked to expressed anger over the American War. The population of Vietnam was young, and Saigon had fallen almost thirty years before. Many vestiges of conflict, like the vast Viet Cong tunnel systems (claustrophobes, beware!) and the herbicide-scorched DMZ, had already become tourist destinations. The legacies of war still lingered—amputees and cripples, barren earth, leftover ordnance—but most people were focused on today and seemed to feel little bitterness over their strife-torn past.

At midnight we left Hue by rail on the Reunification Express. My reserved fold-down berth was occupied by a man feigning sleep. He refused to leave until the conductor came and gave him the heave-ho. Ancient, much-mended sheets and blankets were handed out. The two elderly ladies who shared our first-class cabin were heavily bundled against the cooler northern weather ahead, but five minutes from Hue the air conditioning quit and the compartment turned into an oven. Next door, four drunken men played CDs at high volume and enjoyed an interminable, screeching conversation.

After many sleepless hours, daylight arrived. We were passing through an eerie landscape etched with eroded limestone hills. Our fellow travellers, like many older Vietnamese, spoke a little French, and we learned that they were headed to Hanoi to visit grandchildren and, we inferred, shop up a storm. As expected, the "Express" part of our train's name was a misnomer; we arrived in Hanoi late in the afternoon, hours behind schedule.

Hanoi was a gracious metropolis of lakes and monuments, calmer than Ho Chi Minh City—though the constricted roadways of the Old Quarter, site of our hotel, buzzed with scooters. In medieval times each craft guild established itself here on its own street. The maze of alleys was great for walking; many streets were still specialized, with funereal goods for sale, or silk, lacquerware, embroidery, herbs or musical instruments. At Ho Chi Minh's macabre mausoleum, severe white-uniformed guards made me take my hands out of my pockets and told Katherine not to talk. One evening we were charmed by a water-puppet performance, a Hanoi specialty. As always, we ate well: *cha ca*, a scrumptious fish dish cooked at the table; pumpkin shrimp soup; bundles of slivered pork and carrot, breaded and lightly deep-fried.

Our goal was not to linger in Hanoi but to get back on the water. On a day trip to Tam Coc, women rowed us up the Ngo Dong River and through a series of caves for a close-up view of the karst limestone region we'd seen from the train. This was just a warm-up, though, for our journey's grand finale: an excursion to Ha Long Bay, east of Hanoi. We realized by now the value of paying slightly more for tours. On the bus ride to the boat, our driver neither honked nor overtook; instead, he alerted other vehicles to his presence by flashing the headlights. Our thirty-metre wooden vessel, with eight simple cabins below and comfortable eating and dining areas on the main deck, was the finest in the harbour.

The weather had turned drizzly and grey, which distressed me, as we were about to pass through some of Asia's most striking scenery. But the limited visibility and mist, it turned out, give the bay an aura of mystery. Hundreds of jagged, uninhabited islands erupted from the calm waters in a profusion of cliffs, grottoes and scrubby tropical vegetation. We cruised among towers and pinnacles of rock.

Visits to a floating school and a pearl farm were on the menu. Thuy, our pretty young guide, newly minted from Hanoi University's tourism faculty, led us into an enormous, wave-sculpted cave and, later, up muddy, rain-slicked tracks to the top of a mountain. At night we anchored in snug, sheltered bays, dug into buffets of fresh pomfret and squid, and got to know our European, Australian and South African shipmates over rounds of local Halida beer.

Outside, beyond the boat, we saw no lights. With effort, it seemed, one could escape the din and hubbub of modern Vietnam, which at this moment felt far away indeed. We strained to catch the slightest sound other than water slapping gently at the hull. An older Asia, timeless, surrounded us in the inky dark.

Indonesia 2010

At the Denpasar airport we waited for our luggage. The carousel finally started, and a handsome young porter, resplendent in green-and-white batik uniform and Indonesian *kopiah* cap, grabbed my suitcase. I grabbed it back, with a grunt and a scowl. A gasp of horror rose from a nearby group of porters. Mine looked as if he were about to burst into tears, while his co-workers turned their backs on me. In Bali one was expected to be cheerful and polite at all times. By losing my composure, even for a moment, I had committed a fundamental faux pas. The porters were reminding me that I was a guest in an unfamiliar culture.

It was raining heavily as we were picked up by young Nyoman, our hotel's jack of all trades, who assured us that Bali was always overcast and wet at this time of year. We were staying just north of Sanur, a ten-minute walk from the beach, in a quiet little guest house with a swimming pool and garden, butterflies and birds. Our Balinese-style room was large and open, with a private balcony for relaxing and eating. At the restaurant next door we ordered tasty snapper for dinner and watched darkness fall over our lush green surroundings while lightning stabbed the sea.

The entrance to Borobudur, the world's largest Buddhist temple and one of Indonesia's nine World Heritage Sites.

The next day was sunny and beautiful, despite Nyoman's forecast. We strolled along the boardwalk into Sanur, one of south Bali's many beach resort areas. This was the sixty-plus zone, according to some, and indeed, there was a lot of very wrinkled European flesh on display. Kuta, on the west side of south Bali, had the island's best beaches and bodies, but also its biggest, loudest crowds. It was much loved by young travellers and hard-playing Australian package tour groups. Kuta was heavily commercial, famous for cheap booze, all-night bar-hopping and one of the world's worst acts of violence, in 2002, when Islamist terrorists expressed their contempt for Western values and behaviour by bombing the Sari nightclub. More than two hundred people were killed and hundreds more injured.

Sanur was not so bad (despite the pestering vendors). We weren't there for the beach scene, anyway, nor for the fancy hotels and fine restaurants. We just wanted a place to wind down for a day or two, relax and get oriented before heading inland. That night we ate at the hotel: chicken stuffed with eggplant, fried potatoes, fresh mixed vegetables. The food was better than at any of the nearby restaurants, we discovered, and much cheaper. No wonder the guests never seemed to leave the premises.

A couple of days later Nyoman drove us to Ubud, about thirty kilometres to the north. Shops and small businesses lined the road the whole way. We stopped at the Bali Bird Park; not as good as Jurong in Singapore but a pleasure nonetheless. Plenty of parrots (one tried to remove K's earring) and hornbills. Birds of paradise were a specialty; some ran loose in a big enclosure, and two were tame enough to feed by hand. Large species meandered freely; you could find yourself shoulder to shoulder with a cassowary or a crested crane. No matter how much I loved birds, though, it still depressed me to see them confined.

Ubud was beautiful, perfect for us: trees and flowers everywhere, galleries and museums, classy clothing and craft shops, bookstores, exquisite small hotels, candlelit restaurants and cafés, Hindu shrines and temples. Lots of tourists, yes, but the right kinds of tourists: well behaved, reasonably sober, friendly, appreciative.

If Kuta was selling beaches and booze, then Ubud had the corner on culture. Both places got into the tourism trade during the lull between the two world wars—Ubud as an artists' colony and Kuta as a surfers' paradise. Bob and Louise Koke, an American couple, opened the first surfer-oriented hotel, in 1937. It burned down sometime in the early 1940s, but other establishments soon took its place. A pioneering German painter and musician named Walter Spies moved to Ubud as early as 1927. He helped bring Balinese art and culture to a wider Western audience. Spies recorded Balinese music, hosted visiting artists and anthropologists, curated Bali's museum and co-founded an artists' co-operative. Han Snel, Rudolf Bonnet and Arie Smit, all from Holland, were well-regarded co-op members, as was Balinese sculptor I Gusti Nyoman Lempad. Spies's cottage studio, now part of Hotel Tjampuhan, still exists.

Visitors can stay there if they book far enough ahead.

Writers, actors and entertainers also helped enlarge Ubud's reputation as a cultural centre. Some, like Charlie Chaplin, Noël Coward, H.G. Wells, Margaret Mead and David Bowie (whose ashes were spread in Bali), contributed merely by showing up. Others wrote books about Bali: the Canadian ethnomusicologist Colin McPhee, for instance, lived on the island for years, studying Balinese music and writing *A House in Bali*. Much of Elizabeth Gilbert's *Eat, Pray, Love* was set in Ubud. An annual literary festival had been held there since 2003.

Our hotel had free shuttles, and staff members would drop you in town wherever you wanted to go. This was useful, as Ubud was quite spread out. Walking was complicated not only by heat and rain but also by narrow streets and busy traffic. We cruised the central market, Ubud Palace and the Museum Puri Lukisan (Museum of Fine Arts), home to an impressive collection of modern Balinese art. The work was displayed in a series of elegant pavilions, set on manicured grounds dotted with carvings and lotus ponds. Back at the hotel, we experienced a three-hour rainstorm with massive peals of thunder; lightning strikes seemed to erupt right above our heads. That evening we treated ourselves to an unusual spectacle: *kecak* fire and trance dances, presented by Krama Desa Sambahan, a troupe of about sixty performers. Sadly, there were only ten tourists in the audience, which must have been a bit dispiriting for the crew.

Fifty male singers chanted a hypnotic, ever-varying chorus, designed to induce the "trance," while the major characters, richly adorned, acted out scenes from the Ramayana, a Sanskrit epic of ancient India.

And so our days unfolded. We read and wrote, visited shops and studios, talked to fellow travellers and explored the town's many excellent restaurants (our early favourite, Pundi-Pundi, was set in a gigantic lotus pond). Mornings were best for lengthy hikes through the exotic landscape, as the weather, though slightly cooler than on the coast, could still be punishingly hot.

One of our favourite rambles was through the Sacred Monkey Forest Sanctuary. A band of several hundred long-tailed macaques had taken over this patch of forest. Do not feed these pesky devils! Another good path climbed from a river valley through fields of elephant grass to the Campuan Ridge, with views of rice paddies and 3,031-metre Gunung Agung, Bali's highest peak.

Ubud, we thought, was a kind of paradise, a place we could easily imagine staying for months, working (and eating and exploring). It was the atmosphere that attracted us: the friendliness of the people, the displays of beauty and the attention to detail. No one seemed to be in a hurry. Or if they were in a hurry, they were disguising it rather skilfully.

This apparent slowing of time allowed us to try new activities. I went off to Nur, for instance, a place I'd be unlikely to visit under normal circumstances, for a lengthy massage, seaweed scrub and rose-petal bath. Imagine! At Nur, male customers got a masseur, while the gals got masseuses. My guy, Johnny, was excellent. He gave me a forty-five-minute whole body rub, then exfoliated me with the seaweed paste, hosed me down and covered me in a yogurt-like substance. After another rinse, I spent a final forty-five minutes in a tub filled with hot water and rejuvenating flower petals. Boy, did I smell good.

Katherine and I celebrated an anniversary while we were in Ubud. On February 8, fifteen years before, we'd gone out on our first date (dinner at Vancouver's long-gone Topanga Café). Over the years we had come to enjoy commemorating this event. We also tried to do something special on the anniversary of the date we moved in together.

During that Topanga dinner a strange and unlikely thought had flashed across my mind. It was more like a voice, really, than a thought, and it startled me, because I don't normally hear strange voices. "You are going to marry this person," it said. I almost fell off my seat. I hardly knew Katherine. And note the choice of words: not "You are going to *live* with this person," but "You are going to *marry* her." And I never did. Or never asked, anyway. We talked about marrying from time to time, and neither of us was opposed to the notion, but we were happy with the way things were going. Easier, we thought—and safer—to revisit the idea in a couple of years.

It had occurred to me, though, that if I could summon up the pluck to make a formal but fun proposal, then Bali would be a good place to do it. Was there a more romantic spot in the world to ask someone to marry you? And if Katherine chose not to get married, that would also be fine. No pressure.

We ate dinner at Cinta, a rather posh restaurant on Monkey Forest Road. A quieter, older crowd. I could do it right here, I thought. Go down on one knee in the middle of the room. Not really my style, though ... too dramatic. And I didn't want to spoil other people's meals. Would this qualify as an engagement, I wondered? Did I need to present a ring? Katherine preferred to wear her grandmother's ruby ring. And she didn't bring it when travelling. And nobody got engaged anymore. The more I thought about it, the more complicated the whole thing seemed. Perhaps I'd just postpone any proposals for now.

One afternoon we went to the Ubud Kelod, a large, ornate performance hall, for a presentation of gamelan music and two forms of Balinese dance, *legong* and *barong waksirsa*, performed by a group called Suwara Guna Kanti. The twenty gamelan musicians played mostly drums and vibraphone-like percussion instruments of various sizes. The unfamiliar music sounded alien to me at first, but the more I listened, the more I found myself intrigued by it.

The dancers were spectacular; their hand and eye movements, intense facial expressions and complex footwork mesmerized us. We watched four different dances, including a solo act, where an old man looked back over the events of his life, and the barong, which delved into Balinese mythology and featured monkeys, monsters, dying villagers and a pig costume so elaborate that it could only be wielded by two performers. All the costumes were wonderful.

The next day we left Ubud by hired car and headed to the north side of the island, stopping en route at a couple of heritage sites: the water temple of Pura Taman Ayun and the memorial recognizing the 1946 Battle of Margarana, in which an Indonesian nationalist battalion committed *puputan*, or mass ritual suicide, instead of surrendering to a larger and much more powerful Dutch force.

Our way took us over the mountains, only partly visible owing to clouds. The upper slopes were famous for their steeply terraced rice paddies; a toll was charged to see the best landscapes. As we got higher, vegetables took over from the rice. Heavy rain and thick fog enveloped us as we descended on the northern side of the mountains, but it was dry and sunny again by the time we reached Singaraja, Bali's second-largest city.

We found an attractive beachfront hotel at Lovina, just west of Singaraja, but the beach itself, patrolled by a particularly insistent tribe of female vendors, was not nice. So we rarely left the hotel grounds, where we had our own private gazebo beside the pool. After a tough day of writing, reading, swimming and resting, we'd sneak out to Made, a simple food stall or *warung*, where we had excellent meals and learned a great deal about the personal life of Made herself, owner and chef. I had a "paella" that consisted of a fried egg, a fried piece of chicken, six crispy shrimp and nasi goreng (fried rice). Tasty though.

I guess this was how most people liked to take their holidays—in a tropical paradise, doing nothing. I understood the appeal, but a couple of days was all I could handle, and it wasn't long before we were heading back to Ubud by a different route. This time we travelled via a road that ran partway round the circular rim of a vast volcanic caldera. The ancient depression was wide enough (thirteen kilometres) to have within it another, more recent caldera (seven kilometres in diameter), a large lake, a very active volcano (1,717-metre Gunung Batur), numerous cones and steaming vents, and fifteen villages.

We stopped at a roadside warung for coffee and a long look over this unusual scene. The clouds cleared off and we were blessed with sensational views. Major lava flows (1917, 1926, 1968) had poured across the landscape, while minor eruptions were recorded as recently as twenty years ago. We hated to think of the death toll that might result from a future event.

Back in Ubud, we headed out to Dian, our new favourite restaurant, then watched an hour-long ESPN update on the Winter Olympics, just underway in Vancouver. And so to bed.

We made one more attempt to explore some of Bali's rural areas by taking a hired car to Amed, on the eastern end of the island, pausing en route to walk round the former royal city and regional capital of Semarapura (Klungkung), destroyed by the Dutch in 1908. Then came a long drive on the beautiful Upper Road, through the arts centre of Sidemen and several villages that specialized in snake fruit or *salak*, from a native species of palm. The fruit's outer covering resembled snakeskin, while the sweet, aromatic flesh was crunchy and moist.

We were booked into a comfortable hotel just outside Amed, in a village called Bunutan. As at Lovina, there was little to do. The beaches were black sand and stone. Lots of fish and some coral right offshore, but the wave surge was strong. The hotel website promised that there were no beach vendors. It lied. A whole gang of them were camped in front of our bungalow, watching us like hawks. I was letting the vendor situation get to me, I realized. I reminded myself that it was our presence that brought the touts. They were here only because we were here. We created them. A power outage deepened my self-pity: no air-con, no fan, no internet. But there were wonderful grilled prawns at a neighbouring hotel, while far offshore, dramatic lightning strikes lit up the clouds.

Later, the sky cleared, and that evening we lay beside the pool and watched the stars. Dear reader, you know what happened next. I proposed. Katherine was surprised but pleased. She accepted my proposal. We hugged in the sweltering night and talked about marriage. We would make no immediate plans. With thirteen years of successful cohabitation under our belts, there was no need to hurry.

We decided to go back to Ubud one day early.

Our Indonesian adventure ended with a few days at Yogyakarta, on the larger and much more crowded island of Java, just a short flight away. We were staying at a hotel called the Ministry of Coffee, which I think I chose as much for its name as for its reviews. It was fine, but after a bit of wandering around we found an even better hotel, new, with good Wi-Fi and a nice pool, which would be a bonus in the overpowering heat.

We were in Yogya to visit two nearby UNESCO World Heritage Sites, and also to see the city's palace complex, or *kraton*. Yogyakarta was a "special region" in Indonesia, an anomaly. It had been the capital of one of Java's two main kingdoms, or sultanates, since 1756, and had supported Indonesia's drive to independence during the country's National Revolution (1945–49). As a result, in the modern era Yogya had been given more autonomy than most regions. It was the only part of Indonesia governed by a monarchy, and was famous for its traditional arts (Javanese dance, leather puppetry, shadow plays and gamelan music) and crafts (batik production, silver work and mask making).

At 4:00 a.m., of course, we were awakened by the muezzin's call, for we'd left Indonesia's only Hindu island behind and were now in Islamic territory. It was moving day. We checked out of the Ministry of Coffee and hired a *becak* (tricycle rickshaw) to take us to our new digs. Then we walked deeper into the densely populated neighbourhood that surrounded the sultan's palace and used to be home to officials and civil servants and palace workers. Much reconstruction had taken place in recent years, especially to the sultan's pleasure gardens and bathing pavilion, built in 1758 and known as Taman Sari, or the Water Castle.

Yogyakarta's first sultan, Hamengkubuwono I, took a deep interest in the architecture of the kraton district, which was designed in order to reflect Javanese religion and philosophy. The appearance of the original structures and the spatial relationships between the buildings were meant to remind early inhabitants of their basic responsibilities: to create beauty and peace in the world and to live in harmony with other humans, nature and God. Roadways were allegories: paths one might follow in order to grow in wisdom and compassion, as well as to reach one's destination. The plan or map of the district was symbolic; it revealed the steps necessary to achieve enlightenment. Today, of course, the kraton was very different—and a lot more crowded—than it would have been in the eighteenth century. Now it was next door to Jalan Malioboro (named after the Duke of Marlborough), a major street and outdoor mall that offered non-stop shopping and entertainment.

One morning we rose early, enjoyed our hotel's excellent buffet breakfast and were picked up at seven for a temple tour to Prambanan, one of Indonesia's nine World Heritage Sites. For this excursion we had a driver and a guide, Vita, a pleasant, no-nonsense woman in her thirties who spoke good English. First, Vita took us to Candi Ijo, a small Hindu temple in the hills overlooking Yogya, where it was cool and quiet and she could offer some background for what we were about to see.

The Shailendra dynasty, she told us, emerged in central Java in the eighth century. Its leaders may have come originally from Sumatra; nobody knows for sure. The ruling families were converted from Hinduism to Buddhism in the mid-700s, then back to Hinduism about a century later. There was considerable cultural and religious overlap in the region as a result, especially in terms of temple architecture. Archaeologists have suggested that the construction of Prambanan, so near the great Buddhist temple of Borobudur, which we would visit tomorrow, smacked of competitiveness. "Our towers are bigger than your stupas" was the message Prambanan seemed to be sending.

The temple complex *was* enormous. Built in the ninth century, it was the largest Hindu temple site in Indonesia. A debris field of 224 small collapsed shrines surrounded an impressive group of restored temples at the centre of the compound. These buildings were dedicated to the main Hindu deities and their "vehicles": a swan for Brahma the creator, an eagle for Vishnu the preserver and a bull for Shiva the destroyer. The main structures tapered to sharp points, like stubby spacecraft waiting for vertical liftoff to another planet. The temple interiors were decorated with reliefs illustrating epic stories from the Ramayana. Prambanan was a model of the universe according to Hindu cosmology.

After eighty or so years, the site was abandoned. We don't know why. Because of an earthquake, perhaps, or a volcanic eruption, or a power struggle? Then, for the next eight centuries it was mostly ignored. Much of the original stonework was stolen and reused. Massive, ongoing reconstruction of the site began about 1930, and Prambanan had now been reclaimed as an important ceremonial, religious and tourist centre.

We saved the best for last: Borobudur, the world's largest Buddhist temple and one of the great historic sites of Southeast Asia. I'd long wanted to visit here. We started early again, as the temple was also Indonesia's single most visited tourist attraction, and managed to arrive before the tour buses. Early birds could more easily appreciate the temple's magical setting, in the middle of nowhere, encircled by green hills.

Borobudur was probably abandoned a little later than Prambanan, after another series of volcanic eruptions and the conversion of the people to Islam. It was hidden for centuries under layers of ash and jungle growth, then reclaimed and restored in the 1970s. The temple was a single massive structure consisting of nine stacked levels or platforms. Six were square; three were circular. The top level was dome shaped, surrounded by dozens of Buddha statues seated inside perforated bell-shaped stupas. The main stupa was empty, to symbolize the complete perfection of enlightenment.

If Prambanan's towers resembled space rockets, then Borobudur looked more like a flying saucer (or a huge sandwich). In any case, both sites were equally strange. Borobudur was highly decorated, with more than five hundred

Buddha statues altogether, and twenty-six hundred narrative panels, sculpted in relief. The temple's ambience was one of simplicity—but with an unlimited amount of power available if needed.

Most first-time visitors were so dazed by Borobudur's vast scale that they found little time to study the relief panels, which covered twenty-five hundred square metres and explained, in elegant, sculptural detail, the history and origins of Buddhism, including stories of the Buddha's birth, youth and previous lives. Scenes of daily eighth-century life were depicted, set in palaces and villages, peopled with princes and commoners. The panels had proven a valuable resource for historians, providing helpful information on eighth-century architecture, armaments, vocations, fashions and transportation.

The crowds that eventually formed during our visit to Borobudur failed to disturb its peaceful atmosphere. It would have been difficult, perhaps, to be rowdy as we wandered among hundreds of meditating stone Buddhas. A mood of pleasure prevailed. Children asked to be photographed with us. Indonesian visitors introduced themselves, and we got into a long chat with a doctor and her family from Makassar in Sulawesi. Some of the visitors were pilgrims. The temple was a gigantic mandala that would lead them, as it had led pilgrims for centuries, from the base of the monument, along an elaborate network of stairways and corridors, to the top, passing through the three realms of the Buddhist cosmology: the worlds of desire, form and formlessness.

Many historians believed that Borobudur and Prambanan were built around the same time by rival royal dynasties—extraordinary, really, as the temples were only fifty kilometres apart. The two kingdoms were not at war—not yet, anyway—but seemed to enjoy a peaceful coexistence. Perhaps each king, in a magnanimous gesture, had allowed his adversary to build a temple and promised not to destroy it. Perhaps the two temples became competitive showcases for the kingdoms' skills and specialties. How wonderful it would be, we thought, if all our kingdoms, large and small, could solve their differences in similar ways.[7]

Katherine and Andrew were married in July 2010, at Gibsons on British Columbia's Sunshine Coast.

Turkey 2011

From our modest hotel near the Harput Kapısı, Diyarbakır's North Gate, I set out in search of airline tickets. In eastern Turkey, where few people spoke English and tourist amenities were minimal, making travel arrangements had become somewhat tedious. I wandered into New Town and found an agency that looked promising. An efficient young woman sat at a large desk, and with much hand waving and a handful of Turkish words, I managed to book two tickets from Gaziantep to İzmir. But when I went to pay for them, the computer decided that I was "not authorized to use this international credit card."

Sigh. Turkey is a big place. In two weeks, travelling east and south by bus and train, Katherine and I had already covered fifteen hundred kilometres. Like many tourists, we'd visited the old Ottoman capital of Bursa, been entranced by Konya's whirling dervishes and balloon-cruised the canyons of Cappadocia. We wanted to save precious time by flying from southern Anatolia back to Istanbul, our starting point, via İzmir. Fortunately, I had a stash of US dollars back at the hotel, and by the time I returned to

Opposite:The Mevlid-i Halil Mosque at Sanliurfa, Turkey, built near the supposed birthplace of the prophet Abraham.

the agency, the manager had arrived. He offered me a cup of tea—the Turkish accompaniment to every encounter, every transaction—and booted up Google Translate. Few foreigners came to Diyar, and he was not going to miss this opportunity for a chat.

We sat together in front of his big screen and batted words and phrases back and forth in Kurmanji, or Northern Kurdish. The first word he sent my way, *belengaz*, meant "unfortunate." He pointed to a number of ugly circular scars on his forearm. The second word, *qirkirin*, translated as "genocide."

Welcome to the Kurdish-speaking region of Turkey. Please note that I did not call the region "Kurdistan." If you used this word in Turkey, you had better check over your shoulder to see who might be listening. When we were leaving our hotel in Göreme, for instance, the owner—lean, ex-military—asked in friendly fashion where we were headed next.

"Diyarbakır and Mardin," I said, with enthusiasm. "You know ... Kurdistan." A sudden frost fell over the conversation. Our host's countenance darkened and grew tight with anger. I had no idea what was going on.

"Let me give you some advice," he responded, his voice slow and menacing. "You will make yourselves very unpopular here if you mention that word. *There is no such place as Kurdistan.*"

Okay. I'm all for being popular, especially in places where folk were quick to fly off the handle. I would like to have explained that, yes, from a technical, official point of view, there was no place in Turkey called Kurdistan (though there's a province in Iran by that name). Many people, however, used the word to refer to a large contiguous area comprising southeastern Turkey, northern Syria, northwestern Iran and northern Iraq, where as many as thirty million Kurds—a population almost as large as Canada's—spoke their own languages, followed their own cultural practices and embraced their own history. One often read that this was the largest and most populous ethnically distinct region in the world not to be a separate country (as was intended in the aftermath of World War I, when the Treaty of Sèvres gave the Kurds a homeland in 1920 and the Treaty of Lausanne took it away in 1923). Many Turkish citizens did not like to hear talk of Kurdish independence, and I decided not to share these thoughts with my host.

We entered the Kurdish-speaking region through the ancient city of Malatya, "apricot capital of the world," reached after an interminable train trip from Kayseri and Sivas across the rolling Anatolian plateau. It reminded me of Canada's prairie, but with low-tech farming instead of massive meczed agribusiness. In Malatya we seemed to be the sole tourists, perhaps because it was October. Only sun-dried apricots were available.

We tried to buy airline tickets there, as well, and were even accompanied on our quest by a kind hotel employee, who spoke a little English. We entered a travel agency where a ten-year-old boy sat at the front desk doing his homework. He knew nothing of air tickets. Phone calls were made, but no one was answering. The hotel guy led us to another agency, where a nine-year-old boy played on a computer at the front desk. An unrelated man lounged in an armchair and smoked a cigarette. Nobody knew nuttin'. We were invited to wait while calls were made. The hotel employee fled. Twenty minutes later I was handed a sticky cellphone, and a female voice asked what I wanted. An impossible conversation in quasi-English ensued, of which I understood about five percent. The female voice hung up.

We were beginning to appreciate the importance of the cellphone for sending unhelpful information one's way in a faster and more convenient fashion than ever. After our airline research, for instance, we went to look at a group of renovated Ottoman houses, one of which was occupied by the city's tourist office. We entered and a twelve-year-old boy led us out back, where a man who spoke no English sat smoking a cigarette. Did they have a city map? What? Calls were made. A cellphone was handed me and a voice asked what I wanted. A map? The phone went back to the smoking man and then back again to me. The maps, he regretted, were all gone.

We had no trouble finding our way out of Malatya the following morning. Jolly, tea-drinking truck drivers made us understand that, to catch a bus to Diyarbakır, the largest city in the region, we would first have to catch a *servis*, or shuttle, to the Malatya *otogar* (bus station). This we did, and we were soon on our way southeast, into a landscape that became more and more rugged. The higher mountains we passed through were desolate, but, at lower elevations, irrigated apricot orchards swept down the hillsides to large lakes. This was not an express bus—it stopped to let people on and off—but it was grand enough to provide free tea, coffee, juice and water. After four and a half hours we arrived at the outskirts of Diyarbakır and transferred to another servis, which let us off at a hotel strip near the centre of the city. Looming over the district was a formidable black basalt wall that surrounded and protected Sur, the primordial fortress at the heart of the Kurdish world. Sur was Diyarbakır's "old town."

"Old," however, hardly seemed an adequate description. Sur's layers of human history reached so deeply into the past that time felt irrelevant. Thirty-five hundred years ago a Bronze Age tribe known as the Hurrians had lived here. Then came the Urartians, Medes, Persians and Seleucids, followed by the Romans (who built the first walls), Arabs, Safavids, Turks and Ottomans. Civilizations rose and fell. Many people suffered and died. But different faiths and cultures—Armenian, Chaldean and Assyrian Christians; Sunni and Shia Muslims; Jews, Yazidis and Zoroastrians—had managed to coexist in this part of the world, keeping alive an acclaimed tradition of pluralism for long, peaceful periods.

Then peace turned to war, and people would recommence killing one another. We were visiting Turkey in 2011, the year of the Arab Spring. Major anti-government rallies had taken place earlier that year in Bahrain, Egypt, Libya, Tunisia, Syria and Yemen. On October 20, just days after we reached Diyarbakır, the Libyan dictator Muammar Gaddafi would be dragged out of his culvert, tortured and killed. The situation in Syria, just to the south, was worrying; with the formation of the Free Syrian Army in July, what had started as a social uprising was turning into a full-blown armed insurgency: civil war. But Turkey seemed safe enough. Few people expected the Syrian conflict to become so complex or last so long. Few foresaw that southeast Turkey would soon erupt in military activity and flood with refugees.

We had a more immediate concern, in any case. We were eager to explore Diyarbakır and needed to know if the city's long-running, on-and-off conflict between Turks and Kurds was "on" or "off." In Turkey, if you told people you intended to visit Diyar, many would look aghast. "Isn't it dangerous?" they asked. "Aren't there protests and shootings and bombings and arrests?" That had been the case in the 1980s, when rebellious members of the Kurdistan Workers' Party (PKK), a separatist group, warred with the Turkish army. The government responded by prohibiting use of the Kurdish language and forbidding displays of Kurdish culture. The PKK was declared a terrorist organization. Sporadic clashes had continued until the present day, killing some forty thousand people. But in 2011, though bloody incidents still took place along the distant border with Iraq, Diyarbakır was in ceasefire mode—as safe as anywhere else in Turkey. Demonstrations still occurred, but they were non-violent for the most part; a sit-in of several hundred chanting Kurds was taking place on the broad plaza outside our hotel that very afternoon.

Perhaps I'm romanticizing the Kurds. They are a tribal people, after all: factional, turbulent, impetuous. They treated their enemies the same way they were treated, often with cruelty. They had been implicated in the genocide of the Armenians during World War I.

But while Iraq's five million Kurds had, in recent years, attained a degree of self-government (after being subjected to chemical warfare by the Hussein regime), the seventeen million Kurds in Turkey were still seeking some autonomy. Over the years, they had been subjected—as my travel agent's cigarette burns and tortured memories hinted—to systematic attempts to exterminate them, and they had fought back with all their strength. Many wanted their own homeland, a concept not appreciated in the rest of the country.

We wandered out into Sur, a city within a city—and one unlike any we'd seen before. Circular in shape, with a diameter of two kilometres, a walled circumference of six kilometres and about 130,000 residents, Sur was divided into four quadrants by two vehicular streets; the rest was a mystifying labyrinth of pedestrian passageways and cobbled lanes, made more exciting by the occasional speeding motorcycle or bike. There were few cars to be seen. I had heard that more than fifteen hundred historic buildings had some degree of cultural protection here.

The extraordinary walls, more than ten metres high

and three to five metres thick, hid a network of tunnels, barracks and storerooms. They were punctuated by four main gates and eighty-two watchtowers, many with time-worn inscriptions and decorative bas-reliefs. Only China's Great Wall was more impressive. Some walls were collapsing; most appeared to be secure. From the top you could look south across green fields and see the thousand-year-old Ten-Eyed Bridge, named for the number of arches it threw across the Tigris, a river that issued from the Garden of Eden, according to the book of Genesis. Genesis seemed like the right guidebook for this scene. You felt you were present at the beginning of something: the Neolithic Revolution, perhaps, when mankind moved from hunting and gathering to agriculture and settlement.

Many sections of wall were lit at night and were lined on both sides with walkways and small parks. Beside the paths were the stone tombs or sarcophagi of old Sufi sheiks, draped with colourful fabrics and ribbons and carefully tended. In 2015, four years after our visit to Turkey, we were not surprised to hear that UNESCO had added the Diyarbakır walls to its list of World Heritage Sites. Little did we know what else was to follow.

We roamed at will, and it seemed that anyone with a few words of English would try to talk to us and explain the Kurdish predicament. At the Ulu Cami, Diyar's central mosque (a former eleventh-century Orthodox church, one of many converted Christian buildings in Sur), we met an English-speaking Kurdish veterinarian, who was showing relatives from Iraq around and insisted on showing us round as well. Sur's narrow, stone-paved alleys, only two or three metres wide, were filled with shoppers and bystanders, the women wearing colourful head scarves and long skirts. Fruits and vegetables were for sale, along with clothing and household supplies. Overhead, second- and third-floor apartments extended from the sides of buildings to almost block out the light.

Gangs of overexcited little boys ran wild in the streets. They were amazed to see foreigners and would follow you, screaming "Allo" or "What your name?" or "Where you from?" as loudly as possible. One made a grab at Katherine and I had to push him away. I tried to be circumspect; the last thing I wanted was to create an incident. Most of the kids were fine. Two girls, perhaps eleven or twelve, attached themselves to Katherine. They were a study in contrasts: one gawky and curious, her face as open as the sky; the other with a knowing, world-weary look. They took us to a restored home, now a museum, that we never would have found on our own.

For the first day or two we ate near our hotel. Both of us were fond of lamb and eggplant, so we had no problem with the Turkish cuisine. Turkey is one of the few countries in the world capable of producing just about everything it consumes—a perfect destination for the locavore crowd. Some tiny, hole-in-the-wall restaurants provided a simple set meal. Others offered the usual menu of mezes, kebabs, meatballs, casseroles, stuffed vegetables and rice dishes. People would sometimes ask if they could join us. On our first evening an elderly gent sat down and, in excellent English, told us about his life in America, working at a US air force base. It turned out that his nephew owned the restaurant.

On another occasion, at lunchtime, a man appeared at the table next to us just after we arrived. We suspected that he had been phoned by his good friend, our waiter. He was a retired guide, he said, chatting amiably in English and French—a former government tourism officer and travel writer. He was plausible. We liked him. Then, surprise, he revealed that he had a car and nothing particular to do that afternoon, and we could go with him, et cetera, et cetera. We demurred and he disappeared in a flash. Coincidence—or careful orchestration? You be the judge.

The breakfast buffet at our Diyarbakır hotel was not quite up to the usual high Turkish standards, and we got into the habit of trekking into the centre of Sur in the morning and finding a ringside seat at the Hasan Paşa Hani. There you could have a proper breakfast: all kinds of fruit, a lamb omelette, cucumber, olives, tomatoes, eggplant, yogurt, fresh-baked bread with honey. And tea, of course. How can one live without tea? This handsome, restored sixteenth-century caravanserai—once a meeting place on the trade route to Constantinople—became our favourite stop in Diyar. Many of the city's young people appeared to feel the same way.

The building's central courtyard was dominated by a large domed fountain and surrounded by two storeys of arched alcoves, all decorated in alternating rows of black and white brick. High overhead, broad tarps could be unfurled to protect against inclement weather. Merchants would have occupied the balconied spaces on the second floor, where they could keep an eye on their goods and animals, secured on the ground level. Now the alcoves and courtyard were home to tea shops and cafés, a bookseller, jewellers, and gift and clothing stores. Students worked on laptops, taking advantage of the free Wi-Fi. The atmosphere was a mixture of university campus and medieval castle.

On each excursion we made into Sur we discovered something fascinating: the restored Armenian church of Saint Giragos, now an exhibition space; an education centre, where young women were learning to weave on hand looms; tiny Chaldean and Syrian Orthodox churches that dated back to the third century and were rumoured to still serve tiny Christian congregations. Around one corner: a mosque with a minaret set on four slender pillars in the middle of the street. Down the lane: another caravanserai, the Deliller Hanı, this one transformed into an elegant hotel, its leafy inner courtyard laid out at night for candlelit dining.

Perhaps I'm overglorifying Diyarbakır. I should mention, for instance, that it was a very dirty city. The streets were strewn with rubbish. But the population centres of southeast Turkey had not seen the same investment in infrastructure—in garbage collection, for instance, or sewage and water systems, rapid transit or public housing—as the rest of the country. If you needed an army base to control an unruly crowd, though, you were in luck.

Nevertheless, I could not deny that Diyarbakır was

one of the most fascinating places I'd seen, and I grew fond of it. It deserved, I felt, a kind of respect: after so many years of conflict and pain and destruction, Diyar still survived. It seemed, almost, to be flourishing. So it was with feelings of extreme alarm that a few years later I heard whispers about renewed fighting in the city, especially in Sur.

The collapse of the ceasefire agreement between the Kurdistan Workers' Party and Turkey's ruling Justice and Development Party (AKP) was not widely reported. The first I heard about it was in a 2016 *Guardian* news report by the Istanbul-based freelance journalist David Lepeska. Fighting had resumed in July 2015, after a deadly bombing in Suruç, a Turkish town near the Syrian border, and the killing of two Turkish policemen by Kurdish partisans. In a bid for local autonomy, Sur's militants had seized buildings, set booby traps in lanes and passages, dug trenches and constructed barricades. Turkish tanks and urban assault vehicles responded by smashing their way through the city's narrow alleys. Troops were sent in to flush out the young insurgents. More than thirty thousand Sur residents, wrote Lepeska, had fled in the previous two months.[8]

With a sinking heart I read that hundreds of people had been killed and as many as a thousand buildings damaged, including sections of the historic walls. Aerial attacks had pounded PKK strongholds, while rocket-propelled grenades blew holes in the sides of ancient churches. According to Lepeska, recent video footage of Sur showed "scenes of devastation reminiscent of present-day Syria." Much of the restoration work completed over the previous decade had been destroyed.

The saddest and most ironic aspect of the battle was the fact that the AKP, in recent years, had made more progress toward peace with the PKK than any previous Turkish government. The two groups, both mostly Sunni Muslim, were not ancient, historical enemies. Indeed, the enmity between Turks and Kurds dated only from the end of World War I, when the Ottoman Empire was broken up and Turkish ultranationalists, who viewed the Kurds as backward and uncivilized—"mountain" people—came to power. Policies were instituted to suppress Kurdish identity, undermine Kurdish leadership and weaken the Kurdish community by relocating its members. Political agreements made prior to 2015, however, had eliminated many of these schemes and held out the possibility that the current conflict might also be settled peacefully.

As the fighting tapered off later in 2016, Turkish officials promised to re-create Diyarbakır as a fabled tourism magnet. "We'll rebuild Sur so that it's like Toledo," said Turkey's prime minister, Ahmet Davutoğlu, referring to the restored walled city that has become one of Spain's most important attractions. "Everyone will want to come and appreciate its architectural texture."[9] Voices spoke up to suggest that perhaps this had been the government's intent all along: force the poor to move out of Sur, flatten the slums, disperse their largely Kurdish inhabitants and build upscale housing and tourism facilities. Heritage conservation rules could be overlooked or brushed aside. What this war was really about, claimed the voices, was urban renewal, Turkish-style: profit for developers and convenience for the state. In a 2018 report, Arkeologlar Derneği (the Turkish Archaeologists Association) determined that more than seventy percent of Sur had been destroyed through demolition and redevelopment since 2015.[10] It was enough to make one despair.

The small Kurdish city of Mardin lay southeast of Diyarbakır, an hour's minibus ride through low, gently treed hills. Despite its eighty thousand residents, Mardin had more the feel of a sleepy provincial town than a city, and after the intensity of its larger neighbour, it proved a relaxing place to stay. Crouched on the side of a crumbling knoll, old Mardin was a fine example of medieval town planning: a maze of stone structures in shades of honey and cream, with a ruined citadel perched on top. The Syrian border was only thirty kilometres away.

The minibus dropped us, without ceremony, on the main street in the "new" town. We hailed a cab but the driver had no idea where our hotel was, nor did any of the other drivers at the nearby taxi depot. I prevailed on one to phone the hotel, which promised to send someone to pick us up. Much to the annoyance of our taxi guy, who considered us his fare, the hotel sent a taxi. We ended up paying them both. The new driver gave us an unsolicited tour of the town and ended up in a kind of urban wasteland, where the hotel's co-owner waited. The rest of the way, he explained, our bags would be carried by donkey. Phone calls were made. No donkey appeared. "I will be the donkey," our host clarified. He lugged our stuff up a dirt slope to a warren of paved walkways where we were able to wheel the suitcases without difficulty.

Our hotel was unexpectedly marvellous. I don't recall how we learned about the Kasr-i Abbas, perhaps from another traveller. Bless her! A neat merger and redesign of several centuries-old homes, it had opened only a few months before: seven rooms on three levels, with broad terraces that looked into Syria's backyard, and limestone walls so thick that the interiors remained cool in summer, warm in winter, and needed no air conditioning. The other guests, mostly Turkish, were rarely seen, except for a sociable English-speaking mother-and-daughter duo from Azerbaijan, presently living in Istanbul, where the daughter worked as a translator for the police.

We sat on our terrace, read and drank Turkish coffee. It was a heavenly spot. As evening fell, the weather changed and the temperature dropped. Clouds and distant dust storms rolled in to obscure the Syrian borderlands and turn them a deep blue, pierced by myriad points of light. A full moon emerged. The next night there was a terrific storm: thunder, lightning, wind and a short but massive downpour. By noon the following day the clouds had burned off and the view to the south was scrubbed clean. We could see deep into Syria. Between us and a range of far-off hills stretched a tidy patchwork of yellows, browns and bright, startling greens: Mesopotamia's Fertile Crescent. We could not have imagined that a huge wave of refugees from the Syrian civil war (escalating even then, in 2011, with a brutal crackdown on anti-government protests) would soon wash over this region.

Mardin's civic architecture was even more complex than Sur's, because of the stiff gradient on which everything was built. Stone steps led in all directions, and we paused to photograph fine arches and doorways as we roamed the winding lanes. Many buildings were interconnected, with vaulted passages offering protection from the weather. We learned by heart the 106 steps that connected our hotel to the one vehicular, sidewalk-free street that served the entire old town. Parallel to it stretched a long covered bazaar. Here we met the donkey taxis—working animals, not tourist donkeys—that carried people's heavy goods home from the market, up and down Mardin's steep, narrow alleys.

The city had a trove of extraordinary buildings: one of the smartest post offices I've ever seen, originally designed by the Armenian architect Sarkis Elyas Lole as a home for a merchant family; a nineteenth-century cavalry barracks, now the city museum, also designed by Lole; an atmospheric, historic and totally functional Turkish bathhouse, the Emir Hamamı (massages and saunas on offer, too); several intricately carved minarets, attached to mosques with fine colonnades; a posh governor's house; Assyrian Orthodox churches and monastery; an impressive collection of tombs; some handsome private homes; and *madrasas* or religious schools dating back to the fourteenth century.

In Mardin, as in Diyarbakır, I felt as if I'd entered a kind of time warp. Delete the cars and the cellphones, and it wouldn't be hard to imagine oneself in another century—or another era. I looked out from the hotel terrace at the Fertile Crescent and considered the other cliché in frequent use to describe this region: the "cradle of civilization." The neolithic structures at Göbekli Tepe, for instance, recently discovered not far from here, dated back twelve thousand years; archaeologists were calling them the oldest known temple ruins on the planet. They had been erected by people who were creating, for better or worse, the world's first organized, permanent societies. I struggled to imagine the degree of co-operation that building the temple—with its clusters of huge, T-shaped pillars, many carved with elaborate images of lions, scorpions, vultures and foxes—must have taken. The remains at nearby Nevalı Çori, not quite as old as Göbekli Tepe and now underwater after the damming of the Euphrates River, preserved similar monuments. Nevalı Çori was the earliest site believed to be associated with the cultivation of einkorn wheat, one of the first plants domesticated by humans. The two locations have revolutionized scientific understanding of the Eurasian neolithic period.

The most interesting place we visited in the Mardin area, however, was not neolithic but Christian. Six kilometres east of the city, the imposing Deyrul Zafaran monastery sat alone, protected by a rocky escarpment and surrounded by olive orchards. We approached the building through landscaped grounds, up limestone steps, under a limestone arch, and reached a charming, shaded courtyard. A monastery had occupied this solitary spot since AD 495; before that, the site had been sacred to sun worshippers. For 773 years (from 1160 to 1933) Deyrul Zafaran (also known as Mor Hananyo, or the Saffron Monastery) had been the headquarters of the Syrian Orthodox Church and the seat of the church's patriarch.

Visitors, charged a modest entrance fee, were welcome and could wander anywhere except the monks' quarters. A few monks still lived there. They emerged to greet a German tour group and serve them tea. Second-floor guest rooms were available to pilgrims. Services were held in Aramaic, the Semitic tongue spoken by Jesus—one of the world's oldest languages. In the chapel we were shown a historic throne that bore the names of all the patriarchs who had led the Syrian Orthodox Church over the years. Elsewhere were their tombs, and also those of the church's metropolitans, or archbishops. (In 1933 the patriarchate was moved to Homs in Syria, and in 1959 it moved again, to Damascus, where it is today. The church now has more than two million members, spread widely across many countries.)

With difficulty we pictured this remote outpost as the hub of a global religion, its followers coexisting and co-operating for centuries with Jews, Armenians, Arabs, Turks and Sunni Kurds. But try as we might, we could not begin to imagine such a situation arising today, when so many groups in the region were fighting each other that it was hard even to sort them out.

Three hours west of Mardin was the ancient city of Urfa, known for centuries as Edessa. Urfa claimed to be the birthplace of Abraham or Ibrahim, a patriarchal figure who played important roles as a forefather and prophet, not only for Islam but also for Christianity and Judaism. In the Bible, Abraham was the prototype or model for all believers in God; the Quran called him a righteous example for Muslims to follow; Judaism considered him a founder and spiritual ancestor. Indeed, these three religions (and a number of other, smaller monotheistic faiths) are known today as Abrahamic.

But the legendary figure of Abraham was doomed to disappoint those in search of historical accuracy. His life, for the most part, was a literary creation; it could not be dated to any specific time or particular era. Urfa was not the only place to lay claim to Abraham. A more likely candidate, perhaps, mentioned in the Hebrew Bible, was the Sumerian city state of Ur, now an archaeological site in Iraq near the mouth of the Euphrates.

The lack of historicity in Abraham's story did not prevent Urfa from becoming a major pilgrimage destination. Ur was a lifeless ruin of baked mud bricks, shaded only by a massive stepped temple or ziggurat, but Urfa (or Şanlıurfa, as the city is now officially known) was still very much alive. Gölbaşi and Dergah, the southwestern suburbs of Urfa, were given over to a celebration of Abraham's life: an extensive network of tranquil green pathways connected parks and arcaded mosques and madrasas. One focal point was the Hazreti Ibrahim Halilullah, Abraham's birth cave, where the prophet supposedly hid for the first seven years of his life from King Nimrod, who feared the child would steal his crown.

We lined up in order to view this dank and apocryphal hiding spot. Abraham had been hurled from the citadel by Nimrod but landed safely in a rose garden. We visited both sites. Gölbași was a perfect place to sit and watch people. Many young women wore purple head scarves adorned with silver stars—clearly the latest fashion. Older gentlemen often favoured shalwar: pleated trousers that narrowed to a tight cuff. Families in Western or Middle Eastern garb strolled around two vast pools stocked with carp. The fish were sacred, apparently, and not at all shy; they had grown to a fine size, as poaching was believed to bring divine punishment.

A group of about thirty women passed, dressed in black, cloak-like chadors and niqabs (face coverings). They were led by two young men in smart Western attire who immediately came over and talked to us. "This is our tour group," one of them explained, in good English. "They are visiting all the holy places. We are from Iran. You must come and visit Iran. You would be very welcome."

As at Deyrul Zafaran, we were affected by the intermingling—the blending, almost—of the different faiths and races: Muslims and Christians, of course, but also Turks and Kurds, for Urfa was another important refuge for the Kurdish people (and the PKK leader Abdullah Öcalan was born there). Abraham/Ibrahim was a beacon. All could visit his hallowed sites, pay their respects and receive a blessing. Then we remembered that, between 1895 and the end of World War I, Urfa's large population of Jews and Christians (Armenian and Assyrian) had been either expelled or massacred. How quickly everything could change. How quickly people could be persuaded that yesterday's friends were today's enemies. The contradictions were confusing, to say the least.

Our last stop in southern Turkey was the large city of Gaziantep, or Antep. From there, using the tickets I'd bought weeks ago in Diyarbakır, we would fly back to western Turkey. (We would get to the airport at the same time as a large group of hysterical pilgrims heading to Mecca for the hajj, the required, once-in-a-lifetime visit to Islam's holiest shrine, the Kaaba. The entrance was jammed with screaming pilgrim families, come to see their loved ones off, who were hurling themselves at the doors while security guards tried to hold them back. The luggage inspectors were overrun. We barely got through. Fortunately, the would-be hajjis and hajjahs, clad in their seamless, robe-like, white *ihram* garments, were on an international flight, while we were on a domestic one, and our paths soon parted.)

Gaziantep considered itself the "pistachio capital of the world" and welcomed visitors with a statue of a giant nut. We spent much of our time there eating the best baklava we had ever tried. We also got a taste of what was in store for southern Anatolia. At our hotel that evening we watched the TV news. There had been street demonstrations decrying military activity between Turks and Kurds on the Iraq border. Thirty-two people had died, mostly young Turkish soldiers. The news announcer cried as she read out the victims' names. To the southwest, not far from Gaziantep, the first refugees from the Syrian civil war were crossing into Turkey.

By November, after we'd returned home, Turkey would be setting up camps for thousands of Syrian families. Mardin, Şanlıurfa and Gaziantep were on the front lines. As winter closed in they would be swamped with displaced Syrians heading north, and Turkish soldiers, arms and supplies heading south.

A year later, Turkey would be struggling to look after up to ten thousand new refugees a day. In 2019, according to the United Nations High Commissioner for Refugees, the country was hosting more than 3.6 million "registered" refugees (sixteen percent of Syria's pre-war population) and had provided them with more than $11 billion in assistance. The Syrian crisis, reported Commissioner António Guterres, was "the biggest humanitarian emergency of our era."[11] The COVID-19 pandemic was yet to come.

Japan 2020

On an autumn day in the 193rd year of the Tokugawa shogunate, the cargo vessel *Hojun-maru* left Toba port and set sail for Edo. The *Hojun* was a sizable boat, a *sengokubune*, capable of transporting one thousand *koku*, or about 180 cubic metres, of rice. It carried fourteen crew members, mostly from the village of Onoura in the Owari district.

The clans paid tribute to the shogun after the harvest, and many vessels were heading toward Japan's capital and largest city (known today as Tokyo). Besides rice, the *Hojun-maru* carried special gifts of ceramics for senior officials. The distance from Toba to Edo was about four hundred kilometres by boat, and the journey involved crossing a treacherous offshore stretch of ocean, the Enshunada, where the weather was often stormy at that time of year. The youngest members of the crew—apprentice cooks Kyukichi, aged fifteen, and Otokichi, only fourteen—must have felt apprehension as well as excitement.

In the early years of their supremacy, the Tokugawa shoguns had introduced *sakoku*, or "closed country," a severe isolationist policy that almost eliminated interactions with foreigners. Persistent Christian missionaries, especially, were not allowed to enter Japan. Japanese subjects, if they left the country, even accidentally, could not return. The sakoku laws were in place for more than two hundred years, and the penalty for disobeying them was death. They had a powerful effect on nearly every aspect of Japanese life, including, strangely enough, the design and construction of boats.

Ocean-going vessels, capable of bringing dangerous ideas to Japan from the outside world, were forbidden. The strongly built sengokubune was a coaster, not a deep-sea vessel. It was designed to carry a large cargo a short distance. It had a high, open stern; no keel; a single square sail; a huge, jutting rudder; and a tiller that reached halfway down the deck and needed two men to operate. According to a report of the journey, written by Otokichi several years later, the *Hojun-maru* encountered a typhoon on its way to Edo. "We were blown off course," he wrote, in his understated style, "and we drifted for fourteen months."[12] The boat and three survivors—Otokichi, Kyukichi and twenty-eight-year-old Iwakichi, the navigator—were eventually driven ashore on the west coast of North America, south of Cape Flattery on the Olympic Peninsula. They were the first Japanese known to have reached the Pacific Northwest, and though they missed setting foot in British Columbia, they may well have been the first Japanese to *see* BC (if it wasn't too foggy or raining too heavily). The year, in the Gregorian calendar, was 1834.

The unceremonious arrival of the Japanese sailors had caught my attention some years ago while I was researching a book on the origins of BC's coastal place names. There was a marine hazard called Junk Ledge, for instance, in northern BC, named for a Japanese vessel that had supposedly run aground there many years ago. In 1876, Charles Walcott Brooks, Japan's first consul to the United States, compiled a list of sixty disabled junks that he believed had drifted around the Pacific. Brooks speculated that Asian seamen had been washing up on American shores for millennia, influencing not only the continent's Indigenous cultures and languages but also its gene pool. Later historians discredited both his list and his theories but confirmed that the *Hojun-maru* was one of the very few Asian vessels that could be proven to have drifted all the way to North America.

Japan appealed to me as a travel destination. Tracing the origins of Otokichi, Kyukichi and Iwakichi, and visiting places associated with them, might, I thought, be a way to focus on Japan's unusual culture. I was intrigued by the concept of sakoku and by the way it exerted complete control over trade and cultural contact. Sakoku seemed like an extreme, obsessive version of the "Canton system" encountered in the chapter on China—a system that had contributed to the development of the fur trade in northwest America and, by extension, the settlement and transformation of the region.

The ban on foreign trade and visitors was not absolute in Japan. A certain amount of commerce had always been permitted between Japan and China, for instance. And not all Japanese sailors were condemned to death if they returned home after being rescued at sea or inadvertently grounding on foreign soil. They could expect to be grilled by the authorities and segregated, perhaps for months, but many were deemed harmless and eventually returned to their homes and families. More significantly, one site for regular, official contact between Japan and the Western world was authorized: a trading post named Dejima, established at Nagasaki by the Portuguese in 1634, then taken over seven years later by the Dutch East India Company.

Before moving to Nagasaki, the Dutch had operated a trading post on the remote island of Hirado, about eighty kilometres farther north (now connected to the much larger island of Kyushu by bridge). This post has been carefully reconstructed as a museum and can be visited today. Dejima is also a museum—and a national historic site. It was a strange place in its heyday: a small, fan-shaped artificial island attached to Nagasaki's shoreline by a gated and well-guarded bridge. Buildings on the island included warehouses, and accommodation for Dutch employees and Japanese officials. The services of many interpreters, translators and prostitutes were required on Dejima. The foreigners were watched closely; their personal possessions were inspected; weapons and religious texts were confiscated.

More than six hundred Dutch trading ships came to Nagasaki during the Edo period (1603–1868). They brought silk, cotton and medicine from China and India, plus sugar, animal pelts, books and scientific instruments. The Japanese had copper, silver, camphor oil, porcelain, lacquerware and rice to trade. The Dutch also brought knowledge to Dejima; under their tutelage, the samurai studied medicine, astronomy, botany, photography, military science and various languages. They were introduced to chocolate, coffee and beer at Dejima, and learned to play badminton and billiards.

After sakoku was abolished, in 1854, the channel between the island and the port was partly filled in, and soon there were few signs that the trading post had ever existed. In the 1990s, however, Nagasaki's city government initiated an ambitious rehabilitation program, with the goals of returning Dejima to its island form and restoring twenty-five buildings to early nineteenth-century condition, complete with period furnishings. A large-scale historical model of the entire island was put on display. So far the chief factor's residence (the most imposing building on Dejima) has been opened to the public, along with the ship captain's quarters, the deputy factor's residence, the Japanese officials' office, the head clerk's quarters, the No. 1 warehouse (for sugar), the No. 2 warehouse (for wood), the main gate and the sea gate. Before the project can be completed, a six-lane highway will need to be modified and a channel of the Nakashima River altered. A number of other large-scale urban redevelopments are planned for the district.

My interest in Dejima—and in Japan in general—had been heightened by the fiction of the British novelist David Mitchell, who lived and taught English in Hiroshima for a number of years and married a Japanese woman. Several of his novels take place in Japan; the one that influenced me most was *The Thousand Autumns of Jacob de Zoet*, a love story that so intimately re-created day-to-day life in early nineteenth-century Dejima that I felt I could walk out my office door directly into its narrow alleys. I decided to add Dejima to my expanding travel itinerary. A travel agent was duly consulted about flights and hotels. My wife, Katherine, always game, was willing to come along, and it looked as if my brother David, who had been to Japan before, might be able to join us. But COVID-19 joined us instead. There would be no travel to Japan in the near future.

How could I tell the story of Otokichi and his fellows without visiting Japan? I could write a straightforward chronological account. Or perhaps a counter-chronological one. I'd been to the Olympic Peninsula, at least, albeit many years ago. But another visit south of the forty-ninth parallel would surely still be necessary, and that would be difficult in the short term, as the Canada-US border was closed and the inhabitants of Washington state were having a grim time dealing with the coronavirus. Perhaps I could make a story out of researching the story.

While waiting for inspiration, I read more about the *Hojun-maru* and its crew, fighting for their lives in the Enshunada. A typhoon is defined, today, as a tropical cyclone with winds of 120 to 190 kilometres per hour. At such violent speeds, the first thing to be torn from a sengokubune would be the sail, followed shortly by the rudder. In traverse winds the boat would list dangerously; water would flood into the poorly sealed hold. All the sailors could do at this point to avoid capsizing would be to cut down the mast and throw the cargo overboard. These extreme measures might help stabilize the boat, but the crew would no longer have any control over its direction; they would drift wherever the waves took them. If they were fortunate enough to still have rice aboard, and were able to catch fish and collect rainwater, they might be able to drift for long distances and many months.

The crew of the *Hojun-maru* were not fortunate. They had rice. They collected fish and rainwater. But they could not avoid the perils of exposure and scurvy. One by one, the oldest first, they sickened and died. A few sources claim that their corpses were sealed into ceramic casks or firkins, so they could perhaps at some future point be returned to Japan for cremation and burial. Indications of cannibalism had been reported on other drifting Japanese craft, but the *Hojun-maru*, apparently, was free of this taint. The vessel, pushed along month after month by the prevailing winter winds, was scooped up by the Kuroshio, or Black Current, and carried northeast toward the Aleutian archipelago and Alaska coast. Otokichi and the remaining seamen were oblivious of their whereabouts; they were too far offshore to see landmarks and wouldn't have known what to make of them anyway. The currents bore them slowly east, then southeast, along the edge of North America, to their destination, and their fate.

The Olympic Peninsula is edged with sand and white-veined stone; long beaches line its shores, while flat-topped headlands jut into the ocean every few kilometres. Sea stacks and arches and pinnacles of jumbled rock lurk just offshore, waiting to rip the guts out of any boat foolish enough to approach. Today, national parks, forest reserves and wildlife refuges protect much of the coast, as do reserves for the Makah and Quinault peoples. The peninsula's human inhabitants are isolated and few, but when the damaged hulk of the *Hojun-maru* miraculously showed up that winter on a local beach, the area's Indigenous people were first on the scene. They stripped the wreck of its few useful items—the ceramic gifts, a compass, a necklace of copper coins—and enslaved three barely breathing Japanese sailors.

The unreliability of historical documents, combined with careless research by later writers, has made it difficult to know exactly when and how the next sequence of events unfolded. The Hudson's Bay Company, which served as the region's de facto government at this time, is probably our most valuable source of information. The company kept detailed records, and the HBC archives, located in Winnipeg, are a little-known national treasure, home to 350 years' worth of journals, letters and reports.

The captured sailors, it seems, managed to create a note, with their names (in Japanese) and drawings of a shipwreck and three men bound with ropes. According to John McLoughlin, superintendent of the HBC's vast Columbia fur district (and later known, affectionately, as the Father of Oregon), "the Japanese entrusted the letter to the natives and it was forwarded from tribe to tribe until it came to us."[13] McLoughlin immediately dispatched Thomas McKay, a capable HBC employee, and a team of men to travel overland and rescue the prisoners, but they returned empty-handed, defeated by winter rains and mud.

Another attempt was made, this time by boat. The mariner William McNeill, one of the company's most seasoned officers, took the brig *Lama* from Fort Vancouver (on the Columbia River) to the open ocean, then north along the coast until he located the Japanese wreck. McNeill was able to ransom the captives; he may, in fact, have temporarily taken some tribe members hostage to ensure that the Japanese would be handed over.

On June 9, 1834, Chief Trader Francis Heron, in charge of Fort Nisqually at the head of Puget Sound, made the following journal entry:

> About 2 P.M., we heard a couple of cannon shot; soon after I started in a canoe with six men, and went on board the Llama, with the pleasure of taking tea with McNeil, who pointed out two Chinese he picked up from the natives near Cape Flattery, where a vessel of that nation had been wrecked not long since. There is one still amongst the Indians, inland, but a promise was made of getting the poor fellow on the Coast by the time the Llama gets there.[14]

This promise was kept, and McNeill brought the three castaways to Fort Vancouver, the Columbia district headquarters at that time, where they soon recovered their health. They studied English at a school taught by the Methodist missionary Cyrus Shepard. "While at school," reported Shepard, "they made rapid improvement, and were remarkably studious and docile."[15] They lived at the fort for several months (a fine monument, raised in 1989, celebrates their stay) and caused considerable excitement, as none of the inhabitants had ever seen anyone from Japan before, but McLoughlin finally sent them to London, via Honolulu and Cape Town, aboard the company supply ship *Eagle*. He had great plans for the youthful trio:

> As I believe they are the first Japanese who have been in the power of the British Nation I thought the British Government would gladly avail itself of the opportunity to endeavour to open a communication with the Japanese Government and that by these men going to Great Britain they would have an opportunity of being instructed and convey to their countrymen a respectable idea of the grandeur and power of the British nation. And even if this did not meet the views of the British Government I am certain from the well known philantrophy [*sic*] of the British people that Individuals will be found who will do all that can be done to provide them with the means of returning to their native country. ...[16]

Wrong on both accounts. England was too busy trying to stabilize trade with China to bother bullying Japan, and the company executives didn't care a whit for the future of the drifters. In fact, they censured McLoughlin for spending money on them unnecessarily. After ten days confined to the ship, they were finally allowed a day ashore to marvel at the great city—the first Japanese ever to do so. Then they returned to the *Eagle* for a long journey to Macao in Southeast Asia.

The three "kichis" never touched down in British Columbia, despite coming very close. Who, then, were the first Japanese to visit Britain's far-flung colony? To answer this question we need to refer to "Japanese Shipwrecks in British Columbia—Myths and Facts," a fascinating 2013 article by Grant Keddie, the long-time curator of archaeology at the Royal BC Museum.

Keddie sorts out much of the confusion and misinformation surrounding Asian shipwrecks on the Pacific coast. He confirms that the *Hojun-maru* was the only one of the vessels listed by Charles Brooks that can be proved to have reached the Pacific Northwest. "There is presently no evidence," he writes, "of the occurrence of nineteenth-century Japanese shipwrecks anywhere along the coast of British Columbia. All of the written accounts, making such claims, are based on inaccurate information."[17] The *Hojun*, of course, was a US wreck, not a Canadian one.

According to Keddie, the first Japanese visitors to British Columbia arrived in Esquimalt Harbour in 1858.

They were a group of twelve mariners who had been rescued by Captain Winchester and the crew of the *Caribbean* from their disabled junk while drifting twenty-five hundred kilometres off the coast of Japan. They were taken first to San Francisco, where they arrived on June 7, 1858. Later that year Winchester sailed for China, taking the Japanese with him, stopping en route at Esquimalt, where the refugees, whether they realized it or not, made history. They had not been wrecked anywhere near the west coast of North America, however, and were merely passing through. On January 6, 1859, the *China Mail* reported that the sailors had been transferred at Hong Kong to a British warship, then landed without incident at Nagasaki. In return the ship's captain received "a handsome acknowledgement" in the form of "a Japanese table and some velvet."

The first Japanese person known to settle in Canada was Manzo Nagano, who stowed away on a British vessel leaving Yokohama and jumped ship in New Westminster in May 1877. He was born in 1855 at Nagasaki and worked as a carpenter's apprentice when he was young, refitting and repairing boats. In BC, Nagano fished for salmon on the Fraser River and loaded timber on the Vancouver docks.

In 1884 he returned to Japan, made his way to Shanghai, then sailed to Seattle, where he opened a store and a restaurant. By 1892 he was in Victoria, operating a small hotel and a store, and exporting salted salmon to Japan. He became a man of property, an influential member of the Japanese Canadian community, later consolidating his holdings at one location on Government Street. In 1922, ill and dejected after losing all his possessions in a fire, he returned again to Japan, where he died, aged sixty-eight. Several of his descendants still live in Canada.

And what became of the "kichis," last seen on their way to Macao? They arrived safely, in December 1835, and were assigned to the care of Dr. Karl Gützlaff of the London Missionary Society, who hoped to use the castaways as a negotiating chip in an effort to develop trade and spread Christianity in Japan. He was also anxious to learn Japanese, and his new assistants probably helped him translate some chapters of the Bible into their native tongue. Four more Japanese drifters, rescued in the Philippines, arrived at Macao in 1837 and joined Gützlaff's community.

The British government showed little inclination to help the missionary pursue his goals, so he and his colleagues joined forces with Charles William King, a US trader, who agreed to take the castaways "home" on King's unarmed cargo vessel, the *Morrison*. But much to the missionaries' dismay, when the ship sailed into Edo Bay in July 1837, it was bombarded by shore batteries and forced to retreat. The same thing happened at Kagoshima. No contact was made with Japanese officials, who neither knew nor cared why the *Morrison* had appeared. The rules of sakoku were all that mattered. After years of homeless wandering, the Japanese sailors were understandably upset at their reception. They decided to abandon any hopes of returning home and chose a life in exile instead.

Iwakichi and Kyukichi worked for Gützlaff as interpreters and translators in Macao and Hong Kong, while Otokichi went to Shanghai, where he was employed by the British traders Dent & Co. In 1849 he was hired as an interpreter aboard HMS *Mariner*, which made a cheeky attempt to survey part of the Japanese coastline. According to Captain Mathison of the *Mariner*, Otokichi was in "great dread" of being forced ashore in Japan. "The Japanese would murder us all," he said, "and he would be reserved for a lingering death by torture."[18] The vessel eventually returned to Shanghai. Nobody was tortured. Nobody died.

Otokichi prospered in Shanghai. He married a British woman, lived in a large house with servants and changed his name to John Matthew Ottoson. On his final visit to Japan, in 1854, he seems to have lost his fear of being punished for leaving the country. The fact that he was accompanying, as an interpreter, a Royal Navy force under Rear Admiral James Stirling may have boosted his confidence. At Nagasaki, Stirling negotiated an Anglo-Japanese Friendship Treaty, which, along with Commodore Matthew Perry's forced opening of Japanese ports the year before, effectively ended the country's isolationist policies.

Otokichi was invited to return to Japan to live but decided to remain in Shanghai. His first wife died and he married again, to a Malaysian partner with whom he had three children. In 1862, by which time the bloody Taiping Rebellion was creating chaos in Shanghai, Otokichi and his family moved to Singapore, where they lived comfortably and were treated with respect as cultural pioneers. He died in 1867.

Ironically, back in Onoura (now known as Mihama), the home village of the "kichis," on the Chita Peninsula south of Nagoya, the missing sailors had long been given up for dead. Such a loss must have been devastating for the small community. The families never knew that a few of their men had survived a shipwreck and gone on to live singular lives. In 1832, the year they disappeared, a memorial stone was carved and erected for them in the small cemetery next to Onoura's Ryosanji Temple. Now covered with moss, the script barely distinguishable, the marker still stands; the text can be translated as "Tempo 3 October 11/ Sailed from Toba Bay/Aboard *Hōjun-maru* Jūemon's Ship." Fourteen names are inscribed on the other side. The temple death records also preserve entries for the absent men.

Another monument was set up nearby in 1961, honouring Otokichi for his contribution to the translation of the Bible into Japanese. In 2004, as a result of growing Japanese curiosity about the three "kichis" and their unconventional method of global circumnavigation, Otokichi's remains were exhumed at Singapore's national cemetery and cremated. The following year, a large delegation from Japan visited Singapore and brought a portion of his ashes back to Onoura, repatriating Otokichi after 173 years.[19]

Epilogue

As I researched and wrote this book, I found myself struck by the high degree of co-operation that had once existed between races and religions in certain parts of Asia: Christians, Muslims and Jews in southeast Turkey, for instance; Hindus and Buddhists in Indonesia, Thailand and India. Collaborative occupation of the planet, it seemed, was not impossible—just difficult and unlikely. The East might still have a few things to teach the West.

The journeys I undertook gave me many opportunities to see how people lived in Asia, and to learn about Asian culture and history. To quote Norman Lewis, the famed British novelist and travel writer, I was looking for those "who have always been there, and belong to the places they live." Travel helped me accept the unfamiliar, and pay attention to differences and similarities. Our differences, I began to see, were mostly superficial, while our similarities—the common destinies we shared under the same bright sky—could be profound. Why, I wondered, was it so difficult for us, as a species, to accept one another? And how long were we likely to survive without mastering the basic skill of co-operation?

Most serious travellers, I found, were internationalists. The spirit of co-operation fired them up. Nationalists, on the other hand, appeared to disregard the importance of co-operation. For me, the European Union had been the great experiment in joint international action; Brexit had been the great tragedy. I recognize the need for borders, but prefer invisible ones instead of barbed wire (see the EU again). To risk one's life defending a line on a map—a line perhaps drawn by one group of people at the expense of another group of people—was a sad fate. A flag was just a flag.

All journeys come to an end, of course, though the stories we tell about them sometimes linger. The COVID-19 pandemic, still active as I write these lines (in March 2021), has had a dramatic impact on travel. I hope to be vaccinated against the virus in the next week or so, but I suspect it will be months or more before I pack away my masks and venture back into the wider world.

There were many legendary sites in Asia I knew I'd never get to: Angkor Wat, for instance, or Kathmandu and the Himalayas. Myanmar was once on my agenda. Bhutan sounded intriguing. But there would always be places beyond my reach. It would be boring indeed to have been everywhere and seen everything. I tried not to approach travel as a checklist of destinations to be ticked off and then forgotten. I needed a reason to go (or a companion to go with).

Virtual travel has much to recommend it. Many of the planet's wonders can now be visited in digital form in the comfort of our homes. And the world is better off for it. For most of 2020–21, the absence of physical travellers had allowed nature to flourish. Air and water were cleaner. Wildlife populations were rebounding. Should we not travel then? Or travel less, perhaps? I hoped that some of us, at least, might outwait the pandemic by reading about journeys that others had made. Awesome guides—Bruce Chatwin, William Dalrymple, Patrick Leigh Fermor and Jonathan Raban, to name just a few—were available twenty-four seven to lead us on expeditions to extraordinary lands.

I am fortunate, I know, to have been able to make these expeditions safely, and in good health. I am grateful to all those who helped by providing information, advice and travel assistance, especially the Ceylon Tourist Board, Korea Tourism Organization, Kirk Makepeace and Jade West Resources, Ann Bishop, Michael Wild, Victor George Paddy and Cathay Pacific Airways. And finally, while I recognize that travelling alone has many benefits, some of these trips would have been a lot less memorable had they not been taken with a parent or partner.

Notes/Sources

1 John Meares, *Voyages Made in the Years 1788 and 1789, from China to the North West Coast of America* [...] (London: Printed at the Logographic Press, 1790), 2.

2 "Implications of the 2016 Canadian Federal Government Budget," *National Bank Financial Daily Bulletin*, March 23, 2016.

3 Daniel Hiebert, *Executive Summary: A New Residential Order? The Social Geography of Visible Minority and Religious Groups in Montreal, Toronto, and Vancouver in 2031* (Citizenship and Immigration Canada, July 2012); Ian Young, "Chinese Numbers in Vancouver, Toronto to Double by 2031," *South China Morning Post*, April 6, 2013; Douglas Todd, "Whites to Become Minority in Metro Vancouver by 2031," *Vancouver Sun*, April 1, 2013.

4 Additional sources for the China chapter: Barry M. Gough, *The Northwest Coast: British Navigation, Trade, and Discoveries to 1812* (Vancouver, BC: UBC Press, 1992); John Norris, *Strangers Entertained: A History of the Ethnic Groups of British Columbia* (Vancouver, BC: British Columbia Centennial '71 Committee, 1971); Paul Yee, *Saltwater City: An Illustrated History of the Chinese in Vancouver* (Vancouver, BC: Douglas & McIntyre, 1988).

5 George Thornton Emmons, *Jade in British Columbia and Alaska, and Its Use by the Natives*, Indian Notes and Mono-

graphs, no. 35, edited by F.W. Hodge (New York: Museum of the American Indian, Heye Foundation, 1923).

6 Sri Aurobindo, *Letters on Himself and the Ashram* (Pondicherry: Sri Aurobindo Ashram, 2011), 593.

7 Sources for the Indonesia chapter: Colin McPhee, *A House in Bali* (Singapore: Periplus Editions, 2000); "Borobudur Temple Compounds," https://whc.unesco.org/en/list/592/, and "Prambanan Temple Compounds," https://whc.unesco.org/en/list/642/, UNESCO World Heritage Centre.

8 David Lepeska, "The Destruction of Sur: Is This Historic District a Target for Gentrification?" *Guardian*, February 9, 2016, https://www.theguardian.com/cities/2016/feb/09/destruction-sur-turkey-historic-district-gentrification-kurdish.

9 Lepeska, "The Destruction of Sur."

10 "Diyarbakır ziyareti: Çatışma, yıkım ve yeniden inşa," Arkeologlar Derneği (Turkish Archaeologists Association), January 7, 2018, https://www.arkeologlardernegist.org/aciklama.php?id=31.

11 Kaveh Waddell, "U.N. Calls Syrian Refugee Crisis 'Biggest Humanitarian Emergency of Our Era'" *Atlantic*, August 29, 2014. Also see Kevin McKiernan, *The Kurds: A People in Search of Their Homeland* (New York: St Martin's Press, 2006).

12 Akira Haruna, *Nippon Otokichi Hyoryuki* (Tokyo: Shobunsha, 1979), 30, quoted in Katherine Plummer, *The Shogun's Reluctant Ambassadors: Japanese Sea Drifters in the North Pacific* (Portland, OR: Oregon Historical Society Press, 1991), 103.

13 John McLoughlin, letter dated November 18, 1834, *The Letters of John McLoughlin from Fort Vancouver to the Governor and Committee,* First Series, 1825–38, ed. E.E. Rich (Toronto: Champlain Society, 1941).

14 Clarence B. Bagley, "Journal of Occurrences at Nisqually House," *Washington Historical Quarterly* 7, no. 1 (January 1916): 62.

15 Cyrus Shepard, letter to *Zion's Herald*, October 28, 1835, quoted in Plummer, *The Shogun's Reluctant Ambassadors*, 106.

16 McLoughlin, letter dated November 18, 1834, *The Letters of John McLoughlin.*

17 Grant Keddie, "Japanese Shipwrecks in British Columbia—Myths and Facts," Royal BC Museum, http://staff.royalbcmuseum.bc.ca/wp-content/uploads/2013/08/JapaneseShipwrecks-Grant-Keddie.pdf.

18 *The Chinese Repository* 19 (1850): 510, quoted in Plummer, *The Shogun's Reluctant Ambassadors*, 116.

19 For more information on Otokichi, see the following: Clifford M. Drury, "Early American Contacts with the Japanese," *Pacific Northwest Quarterly* 36, no. 4 (October 1945): 319–30; Stephen W. Kohl, "Strangers in a Strange Land: Japanese Castaways and the Opening of Japan," *Pacific Northwest Quarterly* 73, no. 1 (January 1982): 20–28; Katherine Plummer, *The Shogun's Reluctant Ambassadors: Japanese Sea Drifters in the North Pacific*, North Pacific Studies Series 17 (Portland, OR: Oregon Historical Society Press, 1991).

About the Author

Photo Katherine Johnston

Andrew Scott is an author, journalist, editor and photographer whose work has appeared in publications worldwide. His seven books include *The Encyclopedia of Raincoast Place Names: A Complete Reference to Coastal British Columbia*, which was awarded the Roderick Haig-Brown BC Book Prize and the Lieutenant Governor's Medal for Historical Writing. A new edition of *The Promise of Paradise: Utopian Communities in British Columbia* was published in 2017. Scott lives in Sechelt, BC.